HYPERACTIVITY/ADHD…NEW SOLUTIONS

BY

DR. SHIRLEY LACY

First published by AuthorHouse 10/27/04

ISBN: 0-7596-7733-6 (e-book)
ISBN: 0-7596-7734-4 (Paperback)

This book is printed on acid free paper.

Includes index.

1. Behavioral and Learning Disorders in Children - Nutritional aspects.
2. Attention Deficit Hyperactivity Disorder.

This book is dedicated to my daughter, Lisa Ward

ACKNOWLEDGEMENTS

Writing a book requires the help of many people. I would like to extend my thanks to all those who have encouraged and supported me in this endeavor.

I would like to thank Dr. Bobbie Wilborn, my professor at The University of North Texas, Mr. Ralph McCann, whose donation helped to fund the research; and Mr. Walton Miller, who provided office space and technical support.

I would also like to thank Dr. Stevan Cordas, Dr. F. Batmanghelidj, Dr. William Philpott, Dr. Carl Pfeiffer, Dr. Russell Jaffe, Dr. Kenneth Blum, Dr. Julian Whittaker, Dr. Barry Sears, Dr. Robert Atkins, Dr. William Crook, Dr. Terry Neher, Mr. Al Bieser and Dr. Alfred Libby, who added to my understanding.

Dr. Carl Franklin did a painstaking and thorough job of editing. Thanks so much for all your work.

Special thanks to Carolyn Tartaro, whose friendship, hard work and continuous support actually made this book possible. Without her contribution there would be no book.

The inspiration to do the research in this book was provided by my lovely daughter, Lisa Ward.

Also, many thanks to my late husband, Larry Lacy, for his incredible love and support and for his contribution, the drawings of the blood sugar curves.

TABLE OF CONTENTS

Chapter 1

HYPERACTIVITY

Within the past ten years school teachers, psychologists and physicians have noted that a growing number of children exhibit symptoms of hyperactivity accompanied by learning and emotional difficulties. Large numbers of children in our schools have been placed on Ritalin to help them sit still and pay attention. Some children taking Ritalin do not grow in stature or gain weight. Some continue to have temper fits and are not able to sleep or eat in a normal way.

Carl Pfeiffer has given this description of the hyperactive syndrome:

> The hyperactive syndrome is a disorder of inhibitory mechanisms in the central nervous system which is characterized by fidgeting, inability to sit still, short attention span and impulsiveness. The external stimuli are not filtered by the hyperactive child as by the normal children, and therefore, the hyperactive child is at the mercy of all the external stimuli in his environment. Hyperactivity is a symptom of some underlying imbalance—not a diagnosis. [32, p. 410].

Conners stated that the most frequently exhibited behaviors of hyperactive children were fidgeting, making noises, demanding that needs be met immediately, poor coordination, short attention span, sensitivity to criticism, sadness, daydreaming, crying, disturbing other children, quarreling, quickly changing moods, acting "smart", being destructive, stealing, lying, and temper outbursts [13].

These same behaviors are found in a range of conditions labeled histapenic [32], hypoglycemic [39], and alcoholic [9]. People who have these disorders display aberrant behavior, have food allergies and dysfunction of glucose metabolism. Apparently low levels of serotonin cause them to crave sweets or alcohol.

Studies based upon retrospective information suggest that hyperactivity in childhood is a predictor of later alcoholism [8, 20]. According to these studies and physician's reports of symptoms peculiar to abnormal blood sugar in children less than two years old [25,34], it appears that abnormal blood sugar in hyperactive children is typically present at birth and may be related to a child's craving for sugar as well as an adult's craving for alcohol.

Generally, one will find that close relatives of the hyperactive child are, or were, alcoholic, diabetic, hypoglycemic or depressed. The hyperactive child came into the world with or without attention deficit, dyslexia, perceptual distortion, behavior disorder or anxiety. This child is different from birth. He will not "outgrow" his biochemical individuality. Thankfully, there are now ways to manipulate his body and brain chemistry so that there is more of a balance in the bodily systems that govern the immune and brain functions.

The family and the schools are primary agents in developing socialization and academic skills in hyperactive children. Parents and teachers often become discouraged, however, because the usual teaching techniques may not be effective with these children. To improve learning opportunities for the children and to reduce the tension of adults who attempt to teach them, parents and teachers need to understand the factors underlying the behavior of hyperactive children and to be aware of effective diagnostic and treatment procedures.

The procedure typically used in schools is one of labeling the child "hyperactive" as a result of observations of the child's behavior by the teacher, counselor, and psychologist and the assessment of achievement, academic potential, perceptual skills, and motor abilities. In some cases the school or family physician may refer the child, with consent of a parent, to a neurologist who gives an electroencephalogram (EEG). The EEG can, but does not always, indicate what has been called soft signs of neurological dysfunction. After an evaluation, the child is placed in the class most likely to meet his needs. Even in this specialized learning environment, however, hyperactive children often continue to exhibit behaviors such as restlessness, over- activity, and short attention to tasks, which interfere with learning. They often demonstrate a low tolerance for frustration. They also fight, have temper outbursts and quick and drastic mood changes. Unfortunately, these behaviors often leave them friendless [13].

There is a current evidence to support the hypothesis that some minimal brain dysfunction related to the extreme overactivity of hyperactive children is produced genetically by a subtle dysfunction of a biochemical nature [15]. With regard to the treatment of hyperactive children, then, it would seem beneficial to examine the physiology of this type of child to determine whether or not a biochemical method of remediation can be effective. There are several indicated biochemical dysfunctions which should be checked when attempting to distinguish a hyperactive child. Those biochemical dysfunctions commonly found among hyperactive children which most directly affect their behavior and learning are related to the serotonin level [5, 12], allergic reaction to foods [6,7,33,41], abnormal carbohydrate metabolism [1,2,10,17,23,41,43], need for larger amounts of vitamins

[14,32,34,43], deficiency of minerals [32, 34, 42], inadequate diet [28,29.34.35,37.43], abnormal thyroid production [26], hypopituitarism [26,42], and Omega-3 fatty acid deficiency[40].

One of the pioneers in the treatment of people with behavioral and perceptual disorders using a biochemical approach was Hoffer. He successfully treated over 500 children with learning and behavioral disabilities and enuresis. The symptoms of hyperactivity in these children were alleviated when they took nicotinamide and pyridoxine hydrochloride, omitted allergic foods, and reduced the sugar in their diets [26].

Foods affect the level of blood sugar which is needed by the brain to function, and, hence, affect behavior [23]. In the case where children are found to have abnormal glucose metabolism, it is necessary that they eat foods which enhance glucose metabolism so that their brains will receive an adequate supply of glucose and, hence, behavioral symptoms may be reduced or eliminated[21,38].

Data continues to be gathered regarding the foods, which enhance carbohydrate metabolism. Groen and Cohen have shown that a diet which consisted of simple carbohydrates caused the cholesterol levels in the body to increase very quickly and, in addition, caused persons on such a diet to exhibit definite diabetic symptoms [11,21], which are many of the same symptoms exhibited by hyperactive children [13].

Current research suggests that in order to avoid diabetic symptoms and to keep the brain well fed, the best diet would be one that is void of simple carbohydrates (sugar), moderate in monounsaturated fats with adequate protein, and complex carbohydrates [38]. If not placed on this or another appropriate diet the hypoglycemic or diabetic condition will become worse, causing progressive degeneration of sight, hearing, palsy, and weakness resulting in death [29].

McGeer wrote that neurotransmitters in the brain must be kept at certain acceptable levels or abnormal behavioral symptoms would be experienced. For instance, he postulated that elevated levels of serotonin may cause hallucinations, and it has been demonstrated that low levels cause sleeplessness in animals [3]. Fernstrom and Wurtman have shown in animal studies that ingestion of carbohydrates alone caused tryptophan levels to rise 20 per cent during the first hour and after two hours reached a level of 65 per cent above normal. This elevated the brain serotonin by 20 per cent in two hours. However, when protein was eaten along with carbohydrate, this abnormal elevation of serotonin did not occur [19].

In a review of clinical studies involving serotonin, Coleman found that hyperactive children with normal intelligence had low levels of blood serotonin [12]. The level of serotonin can be raised by administering B6 because pyridoxine hydrochloride (vitamin B6) is directly involved in the synthesis of serotonin (hydroxytryptamine) [5]. Rimland has demonstrated that where 150 mg. of B6 had a minimal effect on the behavior of some children, doubling the dosage to 300 mg. had a dramatic effect on behavior, increasing energy, attention, and speech production [23]. Bhagavan, Coleman, and Coursin stated that, "Available evidence indicates that one of the areas in which serotonin may plan an important part is the system of inhibitory transmission" [5, p. 440]. They further stated that one of pyridoxine's functions is the metabolism of neurotransmitters which are chemical substances in the brain needed to maintain undisturbed sleep, coordinated movements of the hands and feet, and a feeling of elation rather than depression [30]. Further experimentation needs to be done with respect to the effects of specific vitamins and the dosage on hyperactive children.

Another factor to be dealt with in understanding the behavior of the hyperactive child is allergy. Randolph described the allergic child as restless, irritable, unruly, out-of-sorts, high strung, and difficult to manage [36]. He also reported that food allergy in childhood is commonly associated with restlessness, incorrigibility, bursts of temper, drowsiness, depression, and marked changes in disposition. In the allergic child there is a tendency for the eyes to wander and fix on anything. The skin beneath the eyes is often marked by fullness or blue discoloration. He also found the allergic child to complain of headaches, to dawdle over every task, to sleep poorly, have nightmares, and during sleep to grind teeth, talk, and flop around. He stated that the allergic child had inexplicable sick spells, was irritable in the mornings, and could not concentrate for any length of time [36].

According to the current research, the behavior of the hyperactive child is related to a poorly functioning central nervous system and an endocrine system that is out of balance. Growth hormone promotes transport of amino acids from the interstitial fluids into cells, and it is believed that an excess of amino acids then promotes the formation of enzymes and increases the blood glucose level. Corticotropic hormone acts on the adrenal gland causing it to produce more than thirty hormones which govern a wide range of bodily functions, one of which is raising the blood sugar [22].

Medical treatment should establish homeostasis or a balanced relationship between the dietary, hormonal, and nervous system of the body [33]. Testing is likely to reveal low values for thyroid output and abnormal blood pressure [5] as well as low energy content of the electro- encephalogram [32], and abnormal carbohydrate metabolism showing what is considered by some to be poor adrenal output [38] or hypopituitarism [41]. Some children may be found to be depleted of one or more nutrients [32,23]. It would appear, then, that important information to

4

gather on the hyperactive child is: foods to which he is allergic, the ability to metabolize carbohydrates, deficiency or excess of minerals in the hair, a measure of thyroid functioning, and a measure of the pituitary gland's production of growth hormone and corticotropic hormone.

Important information can be gathered by filling out the Yeast Questionnaire [15], and checking items that apply on the Hyperactivity Symptom List, The Conners Parent Questionnaire, Symptoms of Hypoglycemia, and the Feelings Assessment. These questionnaires can be found in Chapter 10 on pages 82-100.

Those who are hyperactive should follow a diet void of sugar, with substantial amounts of protein, complex carbohydrate, and adequate monounsaturated fat. They should take thyroid (if needed)[26], avoid allergic foods [3], take mineral supplements (if needed) [42], hypoallergenic vitamins [14], and Omega-3 fatty acids (found in flax oil and fish)[40].

If the urine is yellow, drink 6-8 ounces of filtered water (depending on your size) 30 minutes before meals, and the same amount starting two hours after meals each hour while awake. Drink water during the night. Hydration (when the urine is free of yellow color) enhances the immune system, provides energy and increases the level of serotonin in the brain [4].

An additional aspect to be considered in developing a treatment for hyperactive children is the knowledge and understanding that parents have about the child's behavior [27,31]. Because of the mobility of our society and the fact that families are often separated from their older members, many parents do not know where to turn for information about parenting skills. The parents of hyperactive children are all the more baffled, as some of the child's behavior seems inexplicable. Parent education groups can provide direct help to the bewildered parents and an indirect service to the child [16]. This is a procedure which can enable the counselor to deal with a very basic problem in the hyperactive child's life—the family milieu.

DEFINITION OF TERMS

Serotonin: A chemical transmitter sometimes referred to as a neurotransmitter, present in a specific amine pathway located in the brain stem and diffusely throughout the cortex. A depletion of this transmitter causes sleeplessness and an excess of it is thought to cause hallucinations [30].

Hypoglycemia: A condition where the blood sugar falls below 70 mg. per cent generally within three or four hours. The condition is diagnosed by administering glucose and measuring the level of sugar in the blood every hour for six hours. Symptoms of this disorder include loss of temper, depression, feeling tense, blurred vision, dizziness, feeling tired, difficulty sleeping at night, needing alcohol, coffee, cigarettes or drugs, suffering from motion sickness, having indigestion, headaches, allergies, fast pulse, and cold hands and feet [23].

Hyperactivity: A disorder characterized by more than ten symptoms on the Conners Parent Questionnaire (See page 87).

Biochemical: The chemistry of living organisms; dealing with the vital phenomena dependent upon chemical influences; specifically with the direct influences and stimuli produced by chemical agents or nerve centers, specific nerves, or cell life [32].

CHAPTER BIBLIOGRAPHY

1. Abrahamson, E. M. and A. Q. Pezet, <u>Body, Mind and Sugar</u>, New York, Avon Books, 1977.

2. B.H.C., <u>Low Blood Sugar</u>, Cleveland, Ohio, Karpat Publishing Company, Inc., 1971.

3. Baldwin, Deane G., Frederick J. Kittler, and Reginald C. Ramsay, Mr., "The Relationship of Allergy to Cerebral Dysfunction", <u>Southern Medical Journal</u>, LXI (October, 1968), 1039-1041.

4. Batmanghelidj, F., "Pain: A Need for Paradigm Change", <u>Anticancer Research</u>, (July, 1987), 971-990.

5. Bhagavan, Hemmige N., Mary Coleman, and David Baird Coursin, "The Effect of Pyridoxine Hydrochloride on Blood Serotonin and Pyridoxal Phosphate Contents in Hyperactive Children". <u>Pediatrics</u>, LV (March, 1975), 437-441.

6. Breneman, James C., "Allergic Cystitis: The Cause of Nocturnal Enuresis". <u>General Practitioner</u>, XX (December, 1959), 85-98.

7. Bryan, W. T. and K. Bryan, "Cytotoxic Reactions in the Diagnosis of Food Allergy", <u>Laryngoscope</u>, LXXXIX (1969), 1453-1472.

8. Cantwell, D. P., "Psychiatric Illness in the Families of Hyperactive Children", <u>Archives of General Psychiatry</u>, LSS (1072), 414-417.

9. Cheraskin, E., <u>Psychodietetics</u>, New York, Stein and Day Publishers, 1974, p. 192-194.

10. Cheraskin, E., and W. M. Ringsdorf, Jr., <u>Diet and Disease</u>, New Canaan, Connecticut, Keats Publishing Inc., 1968.

11. Cohen, A. M., Alisa Teilejbaum, Miriam Balogh, and J. J. Groen, "Effect of Interchanging Bread and Sucrose as Main Source of Carbohydrate in a Low Fat Diet on the Glucose Tolerance Curve of Healthy Volunteer Subjects", <u>American Journal of Clinical Nutrition</u>, XIX (1966), 59-62.

12. Coleman, Mary, "Serotonin and Central Nervous System Syndromes of Childhood: A Review", <u>Journal of Autism and Childhood Schizophrenia</u>, III (1973), 27-35.

13. Conners, C. Keith, <u>Conners Parent Questionnaire</u>, Form No. 68-R965, Department of Health, Education and Welfare, Health Services, and Mental Health Administration, National Institute of Mental Health, 1976.

14. Cott, A. Allen, "A Hyperactive Child Needs Nutrients, Not Drugs", Prevention, April, 1971, p. 169-176.

15. Crook, William G., The Yeast Connection Handbook, Professional Books, P. O. Box 3246, Jackson, Tennessee 38302, 1996.

16. Davis, Richard E., "Manic Depressive Variant of Childhood: A Preliminary Report", American Journal of Psychiatry, CXXXVI (May, 1979), 702-706.

17. Dinkmeyer, Don and Gary D. McKay, Systematic Training for Effective Parenting, American Guidance Service, Inc., Circle Pines, Minnesota 55014, 1976.

18. Duncan, Garfield G., Diseases of Metabolism, Philadelphia, W. B. Saunders Company, 1952.

19. Ekins, R. P., E. S. Williams, and S. Ellis, "The Sensitive and Precise Measurement of Serum Thyroxine by Saturation Analysis (Competitive Protein Binding Assay)", Clinical Biochemistry, (1969), 253.

20. Fernstrom, John D. and Richard J. Wurtman, "Nutrition and the Brain", Scientific American, CCXXX (February, 1974), 84-91.

21. Goodwin. Donald W., Fini Schulsinger, Leif Hermansen, Samuel B. Guze, and George Winokur, "Alcoholism and the Hyperactive Child Syndrome", The Journal of Nervous and Mental Disease, CLX (May, 1975), 349-353,

22. Groen, J. J., M. Balogh. and A. M. Cohen, "Effect of Interchanging Bread and Sucrose as Main Source of Carbohydrate on Cholesterol Level", American Journal of Clinical Nutrition, XIX (1966), 46-58.

23. Hawkins, David, Linus Pauling, Orthomolecular Psychiatry Treatment of Schizophrenia San Francisco, W. H. Freeman and Company, 1973.

24. Henderson, Lana, "The Hyperactive Child: Inside the Playground of a Busy Mind", Sunday Magazine the Dallas Times Herald, February 23, 1975.

25. Hill, James R., Personal interview in Dallas, Texas.

26. Hoffer, Abram, Schizophrenia, Cleveland, Ohio, Karpat Publishing Company, Inc. 1972.

27. Kessler, J., Psychopathology of Childhood, Englewood Cliffs, New Jersey, Prentice Hall. 1966.

28. Kiem, Joe G., James and Kyleen Ward, "Beneficial Effect of a High Carbohydrate, High Fiber Diet on Hyperglycemic Diabetic Men", <u>American Journal of Clinical Nutrition</u>, XXIX (1976), 895-899.

29. Leonard, Jon N., Jack L. Hofer, and Nathan Pritikin, <u>Live Longer Now</u>, New York, Grossett and Dunlap, 1974.

30. Geer, Patrick L., "The Chemistry of Mind", <u>American Scientist</u>, LIX (March-April, 1971), 221-229.

31. Patterson, G. R., "Interventions for Boys with Conduct Problems", <u>Journal of Counseling and Clinical Psychology</u>, XLI (1974), 15.

32. Pfeiffer, Carl C., <u>Mental and Elemental Nutrients</u>, New Canaan, Connecticut, Keats Publishing, Inc., 1975.

33. Philpott, W. H., "The Significance of Selected Food and Chemical Stressors in Ecological Hypoglycemia and Hyperglycemia", <u>Journal: International Academy of Metabology, Inc.</u>, V (May, 1967), 36-41.

34. Powers, Hugh W. W., Personal interview in Dallas, Texas.

35. Rabinowitch, I. M., "The Effects of High Carbohydrate - Low Calorie Diet upon Carbohydrate Tolerance in Diabetes Mellitus", <u>The Canadian Medical Association Journal</u>, XXXIII (August, 1935), 136-144.

36. Randolph, Theron G., "Allergy as a Causative Factor of Fatigue, Irritability, and Behavior Problems of Children", <u>Journal of Pediatrics</u>, XXXI (July-December, 1947), 560-572.

37. Ringsdorf, W. M., Jr., E. Cheraskin, and R. R. Ramsay, Jr., "Sucrose, Neutrophilic Phagocytosis and Resistance to Disease", <u>Dental Survey</u>, LII (December, 1976), 46-48.

38. Sears, Barry, <u>Enter the Zone</u>, New York City, New York, Metabolic Research Society, 1974.

39. Springer, Ninfa S. and Norma L. Fricke, "Nutrition and Drug Therapy for Persons with Developmental Disabilities", <u>American Journal of Mental Deficiency</u>, LXXX (1975), 317-322.

40. Stevens, Laura, et al, "Essential Fatty Acid Metabolism in Boys with Attention-Deficit Hyperactivity Disorder", <u>American Journal of Clinical Nutrition</u>, 62, (1995), 761-768.

41. Tintera, John, <u>Hypoadrenocorticism,</u> Mt. Vernon, New York, Metabolic Research Society, 1974.

42. Williams, Roger and Dwight Kalita, <u>A Physician's Handbook on Orthomolecular Medicine</u>, New York, 1977.

43. Wunderlich, Ray C., "Paranoid Schizophrenia as a Manifestation of Metabolic Derangement: Successful Management by Metabolic Therapy", <u>Journal of the International Academy of Preventive Medicine</u>, III (September, 1976), 21-36.

44. Wunderlich, Ray C., "The Hyperactivity Complex", <u>Journal of Optometric Vision Development</u>, VIII (March, 1977), 8-45.

Chapter 2

REVIEW OF THE LITERATURE

Contributors to the medical literature have found that hyperactive ADHD children have abnormalities and imbalances in body chemistry. These are not, on the whole, permanent conditions, but they can be manipulated. Hyperactive children have been found to have abnormally low hydroxyindoles (which reflected serotonin content) in the blood[11]. This low level of serotonin may be behaviorally demonstrated by inability to pay attention and sleep disturbance[28]. Bhagavan, Coleman, and Coursin found that four to forty milligrams of B6 per day elevated serotonin levels into the normal range on hyperactive children studied [5].

A team of researchers at the National Institute of Mental Health found impulsive, aggressive behavior to be associated with low levels of serotonin and high levels of norepinephrine. The study included twenty-five enlisted men who had poor impulse control, poor judgment, temper tantrums and exhibited aggression. According to Brown, men with the most aggressive histories had the lowest levels of serotonin and the highest levels of norepinephrine [7].

Allergic reaction to certain foods is another factor which has been found to be related to hyperactivity in children. These allergic reactions, due to inability of the body to break down the food because of lack of hormones, hydrochloric acid, and enzymes [35,47], cause the white cell count to drop [9] thereby inducing illness in the form of fever, aching, sore throat, and exhaustion [46]. Allergic reactions to food also may bring about a drop in blood sugar, a rise in blood pressure and behavioral symptoms such as withdrawal from people, anger, lying, depression, loss of memory, and suicide attempts [45]. Breneman reported that a complete reversal of hostility and aberrant behavior and cessation of nocturnal enuresis was observed in hyperactive children when allergic foods were eliminated from the diet [6].

Baldwin, Kittler, and Ramsay studied twenty children with severe learning problems, allergy, and abnormal electroencephalograms who were treated for their allergy by avoidance measures. Following treatment, nine had normal electroencephalograms, two had questionably improved electroencephalograms, and no change was seen in the rest [3].

Philpott presented a case study which further clarified the abnormal behavior caused by food allergy. After a four day fast, Philpott administered several foods to a thirty year old man with manic depressive symptoms. Before the test for cream cheese the man was symptom free. Within thirty minutes after eating cream cheese, he fluctuated between extreme fright of environmental stimuli and a comatose state of no response to sight and sound stimuli. His pulse was 123 and his blood pressure 170/110. At this point his blood sugar was 20 mg. per cent. He was given vitamin C (12.5 grams), B6 (1000 mg.), calcium gluconate (10 cc), magnesium sulphate (2 grams), adrenal cortical extract (20 cc). After this treatment he awakened, was communicative, understood, and was not frightened by environmental stimuli. His pulse was 80 and his blood pressure was 130/84. He was given six teaspoons of beet sugar, a glass of pineapple juice, and several bites of chocolate cake. Within thirty minutes his blood sugar was 160 mg. per cent, and he was symptom free [35].

Crook has described the allergic child as overactive, clumsy, irritable, oversensitive, tired, and complaining. He says that such a child may be hypersensitive to pain, noise, and light, sometimes having irrational behavior and paranoid ideas. Pallor, headaches, nasal stuffiness, abdominal pain, and enuresis also may be part of the allergic child's symptoms. Crook states that of the allergic children he treated in 1973, ninety-one percent of the children partially or totally lost the symptoms they had when allergenic foods were avoided [16].

Bell defines ecological illness as a variety of chronic syndromes which result from multiple sensitivities to substances from the external environment, such as foods and chemicals, as well as natural inhalants. She describes the allergic person as one who is engulfed with emotions such as anger, resentment, helplessness, depression, and thoughts of suicide [4].

A third factor to be considered in the study of hyperkinetic children is carbohydrate metabolism. Persons with abnormal carbohydrate metabolism are said to be hypoglycemic, pre-diabetic or diabetic depending on the blood sugar curve exhibited during a six hour glucose tolerance test [22]. The electroencephalogram of a person with hypoglycemia differs from that of a normal person. In the past, an abnormal EEG was thought to be due to insult to the brain, however, one current study shows that with effective treatment of hypoglycemia the brain wave returned to normal [3]. The brain relies almost exclusively on circulating blood glucose as its energy source [43]. As long as the blood sugar stays within normal limits the nervous system is well fed [19]. Wunderlich states that blood sugar levels between 80 and 89 mg. per cent appear to be associated with more optimal metabolism and better adaptation to the stresses of daily living [47]. Abrahamson says normal limits for the third and fourth hour sample lie between 80 and 110 milligrams per 100 cc of blood [1]. Symptoms presented by a person whose blood sugar is out of the normal range are visual disturbances, headaches, fatigue, depression, mood swings, tantrums, nausea, dizziness, and ringing in the ears [19,33,47]. Another problem associated with high blood sugar is that the number of phagocytes (leucocytes which destroy harmful bacteria such as Staphylococcus) are reduced to a point where susceptibility to disease is increased [40].

Tintera reported seventeen cases of disordered carbohydrate metabolism accompanied by various mental and emotional disturbances [45]. Symptoms of these patients improved or disappeared with a hypoglycemic diet (which was high protein, low carbohydrate), adrenal cortical extract, B6, B12, Bellergal Spacetabs and sometimes thyroid, testosterone, estrogen or progesterone.

Wunderlich reported the treatment of a girl who was depressed, frightened, had mood swings, withdrawn and also had nausea, vomiting, and abdominal pain, crying spells, and sleep disturbance. This girl had disordered carbohydrate metabolism which he classed as a diabetic blood sugar curve. Her hair analysis showed that she was high in cadmium and low in calcium, magnesium, sodium, iron, and manganese. She showed poor digestion of starch and inadequate production of hydrochloric acid. She was treated with low doses of minerals, niacinamide, pyridoxine, ascorbic acid, one multiple vitamin, oral hydrochloric acid, a low level microendocrine pituitary supplement, and a diet in which all sugar, refined carbohydrates, and processed foods were eliminated. Wheat, citrus fruits, and milk were eliminated from the diet and she was given injections of B12 and iron. Improvement was gradual, and in five months she had a more optimal glucose tolerance curve. Her hair analysis was closer to normal, her mental symptoms disappeared, and she was able to return to regular school [48].

Pfeiffer states that some patients who have low blood pressure, headache, dizziness, sweating, nausea, and feelings of unreality also have abnormal carbohydrate metabolism (or a flat or hypoglycemic blood sugar curve). Specific foods affect the ability of the body to metabolize carbohydrates. According to Pfeiffer, candy, ice cream, doughnuts, soft drinks, and other confections lead to the development of hypoglycemia and diabetes [33]. He says that the disorder usually responds very well to a high protein and low sugar diet [34].

Pfeiffer states that many of the B vitamins function as enzymes in carbohydrate metabolism. In addition, trace elements are essential for carbohydrate metabolism. He says effective metabolism is the keystone for proper function of nerve cells and tissues [33].

More optimal functioning in hyperkinetic children has been observed following large doses of B6, pantothenic acid, B-complex, folic acid, niacinamide, vitamin C, and B12 [13,33,37,47]. Pfeiffer found that 100 milligrams of thiamin and 1000 milligrams of ascorbic acid have an antianxiety or sedative effect, characterized by a significant decrease in the mean "energy content" of the electroencephalogram [33].

In a study of 300 children, Rimland collected data on the effects of large doses of vitamin C, B6, pantothenic acid on the behavior of children. Parents reported that the children displayed more cooperative behavior and exhibited dramatic improvement in energy, alertness, and speech production [22].

The hyperkinetic child has been labeled, "histapenic", by Pfeiffer. He found this type of individual to have low blood levels of histamine. Symptoms were removed with a treatment of vitamin C, niacin, folic acid, and weekly B12 injections [33].

Cott prescribed vitamins for children with behavior and learning disorders. He found that as a result of taking vitamins children became more normal in both areas [13].

Mineral elements such as calcium, magnesium, sodium, potassium, copper, zinc, iron, manganese, selenium, cobalt, molybdenum, and chromium may be deficient, excessive or imbalanced in hyperactive children [33,37]. When a favorable balance in these elements is obtained, significant improvement in the hyperactivity complex can occur [47].

An apparent link between learning disabilities and abnormally high lead and cadmium levels in children has been established by Pihl, who reported almost uniformly elevated lead and cadmium levels in thirty-one learning disabled children with problems in language, comprehension, motor skills, and orientation. Both lead and cadmium were substantially elevated in the hair of learning disabled children. Much lower values were found in normal youngsters. While lead has already been linked to hyperactivity, this is the first study to implicate lead in learning disabilities [36].

One trace mineral, chromium, is a necessary catalyst in order for the pancreatic hormone, insulin, to fulfill its function of inducing the uptake of glucose from the bloodstream by the cells of the body [38]. Mertz has shown that chromium can be used with humans who are deficient in chromium to help maintain optimal metabolism [24].

Potassium loss is typically found in diabetics. Potassium can be replenished with foods such as bananas, pineapples, pecans, buckwheat, and navy beans which have rich potassium content or by taking potassium supplements.

Zinc is essential to the proper functioning of insulin, According to Kuhnau and von Holt, zinc is necessary for the functional integrity of the B-cells in the pancreas which secrete insulin. Without adequate zinc the cells that secrete insulin are impaired in their function and their structure and form are threatened [24]. Zinc is concentrated in larger amounts in the hippocampus than in other areas of the brain. By means of polyneuronal connections with the neocortex and hypothalamic nuclei, the hippocampus has the potential for strongly influencing behavioral and visceromatic activities in the body. The hippocampus participates in memory processing and modulation of neuroendocrine secretions via the hypothalamus and the hippocampus is responsive to circulating hormones. Stimulation in hippocampal areas evokes responses in the cardiovascular, gastrointestinal, and genitourinary systems [15].

Six of the ten enzymes in the glycolytic pathway are activated by magnesium according to Wunderlich. He says that it is estimated that 78 per cent of the enzyme reactions in the body are catalyzed by magnesium [47].

Hyperactive children typically have inadequate diets and frequently eat large quantities of sugared food [37,47]. This habitual behavior impairs glucose metabolism [39]. Presently there is a trend among some professionals to use diet to alter behavior.

Fernstrom[20] has shown in animal experimentation that dietary constituents influence neurotransmitters serotonin and acetylcholine. Low levels of serotonin cause sleep disturbance [29] and sensitivity to pain [20] and acetylcholine is found in the hippocampus, a region of the brain important in learning and memory. Both lecithin and choline cause increased amounts of acetycholine in the brain [20].

Researchers using the Feingold Diet found it to be effective with hyperkinetic children. Conners and Goyetter [12] tested fifteen children, evaluating each child on a regular diet and then on the Feingold Diet. Teachers reported fewer hyperkinetic symptoms for children on the Feingold Diet compared to their pre-treatment behavior.

In a study at North Texas State University, ten hyperactive children were tested with an actometer, a device used to measure the amount of arm and leg movement to determine levels of hyperactivity [41]. The children placed on the Feingold Diet measured 168 actometer units per minute when treatment began and 97 when it ended. The control group of five children not on the diet began with an average of 155 actometer and completed with 147.

Confirmation of the Feingold theory at the molecular level comes from research at the University of Maryland. Levitan [27] has shown that food dyes cut down on responses of nerves and muscles to signals from other nerves.

Pritikin [26] states that to avoid hypertension, heart attack, diabetes and atherosclerosis, it is necessary to pay attention to the food that is eaten. To avoid the build up of plaques in the arteries one should avoid fatty meats, oils, dairy products, sugar, honey, syrup, pies, cakes, and pastries. He advises that people should not use additional salt when cooking. Meat should be limited to one quarter pound of lean meat per day. Organ meats should be avoided and coffee and tea should be replaced with herb tea and water. Using his diet, which is void of simple carbohydrates, low in fat, moderate in protein and high in complex carbohydrates, these dangerous conditions can be avoided [26].

Anderson has shown that diabetic men who were fed a diet of seventy-five per cent carbohydrate, low fat, moderate protein, and fifteen grams of crude dietary fiber had more optimal curves on their glucose tolerance tests [25]. He also showed that non-diabetic or normal subjects had a better curve on glucose tolerance tests if they replaced the sugar in their diet with bread [10]. Complex carbohydrates have a positive effect on carbohydrate metabolism (the curve of the glucose tolerance test), whereas simple carbohydrates such as sugar have the opposite affect.

Recently, Dr. Barry Sears has shown that high carbohydrate diets are not healthy. He has demonstrated that a diet composed of approximately 30% protein, 40% complex carbohydrate and 30% fat prevents the production of excessive insulin, heart disease, diabetes and perhaps cancer. Eating protein, carbohydrate and fat at the same time allows optimal brain functioning and energy levels. Swimmers and basketball players found that eating in "the Zone" provided them with greater strength and endurance [42].

Some hyperactive children have been reported to have abnormal thyroid functioning. Hyperkinetic symptomatic behavior has improved when children received thyroid [23]. Asher described hypothyroidism ("Myxoedema madness") as organic brain syndrome. He said that in addition to the signs and symptoms of brain impairment, delusions and auditory hallucinations may occur, usually persecutory, though sometimes with a depressive flavor [2].

One physician reported a case study of a woman, age twenty-seven. The woman had suffered from a chronic state of depression exhaustion, and auditory hallucinations. Results of the routine thyroid function tests were normal, but she had a defective TSH (thyrotropin stimulating hormone) response to a TRH (thyrotropin releasing hormone) load. Treatment with thyroid hormones produced a rapid and permanent amelioration of her symptoms [30].

Pathological overactivity of the thyroid almost always produces some psychological disturbances. The disturbance can range from a constant state of anxiety to acute delirium [44]. The professional dealing with behavior disturbance must wonder whether or not subtle changes in thyroid function may also influence mental state [14].

Some children with blood sugar disorders also have hypopituitarism. According to Brown, patients with hypopituitarism frequently become dependent, apathetic, depressed, drowsy, lose their drive and initiative, and are fatigued. Their mental symptoms range from confusion to frank psychosis [8].

Page indicates that pituitary deficiency is often associated with mental illness, fatigue, and depression. He points out that disturbed menstrual and reproductive functions in the female are often improved by treatment with pituitary hormone in micro-doses [32].

Wunderlich used a treatment of an oral, low level, microendocrine, pituitary supplement and observed an improvement in physical stamina and weight gain. Symptoms of nausea and dizziness disappeared. Menstrual cycles became more normal, and the patient only rarely had stomach aches [48]. Hoffer treated a patient with a blood sugar abnormality adding hormones to his usual treatment of diet and vitamins and observed a reduction in angry behavior [23].

Insufficient amounts of pituitary hormones are thought by some physicians to be the reason for late births and long deliveries [31,48]. There is reason, then, to suspect that children born past the full term may have an insufficient supply of pituitary hormones [48].

Daughaday feels that plasma levels of growth hormone, a hormone secreted by the pituitary gland, are related to the diabetic condition. Growth hormone releasing factor (GHRF), produced in the hypothalamus, causes the release of the GH. In one study, low blood sugar was induced resulting in an outpouring of growth hormone after ten to twenty minutes. Conversely, when glucose was administered to individuals the level of growth hormone fell promptly [17]. Since it has been established that eating sugars and fats interferes with carbohydrate metabolism [26] and that because of this kind of eating blood sugar fluctuates, then the result would be a fluctuation of the growth hormone. Optimal levels of growth hormone are needed as this hormone causes growth of cells, elevation of blood glucose level, and the production of enzymes which break up food [21].

Summary

There is a growing body of data indicating that the hyperkinetic syndrome is genetically produced [18] and that it involves subtle biochemical imbalances [11,18,34,47]. Various studies have found specific biochemical abnormalities common to hyperactive children. The abnormalities included a low level of serotonin [11], allergy to food [16], abnormal carbohydrate metabolism mineral imbalance [18], and need for extra vitamins and minerals [13,14]. Imbalances in the production of hormones by the pituitary [32] and the thyroid gland [2] have been known to cause abnormal behavior and physiological symptoms. A diet which is void of sugar and caffeine, moderate in protein and carbohydrate with adequate fat is the diet which will promote optimal carbohydrate metabolism [42] and, hence, behavior void of symptomology. Barry Sears in Mastering the Zone and The Omega Rx Zone has demonstrated that his suggestions for eating control blood sugar and produce energy.

CHAPTER BIBLIOGRAPHY

1.   Abrahamson, E. M. and A. Q. Pezet, <u>Body, Mind and Sugar</u>, New York, Avon Books, 1977.

2.   Asher, R., <u>British Medical Journal</u>, II (1949), 555.

3.   Baldwin, Deane G., Frederick J. Kittler, and Reginald C. Ramsay, Jr., "The Relationship of Allergy to Cerebral Dysfunction", <u>Southern Medical Journal</u>, LXI (October, 1968), 1039-1041.

4.   Bell, Iris R., "Ecologic Illness: The Experience", FCPM 274, unpublished paper, Stanford University School of Medicine, November 8, 1976.

5.   Bhagavan, Hemige N., Mary Coleman, and David Baird Coursin, "The Effect of Pyridoxine Hydrochloride on Blood Serotonin and Pyridoxal Phosphate Contents in Hyperactive Children", <u>Pediatrics</u>, LV (March, 1975), 437-446.

6.   Breneman, James C., "Allergic Cystitis: The Cause of Nocturnal Enuresis", <u>General Practitioner</u>, XX (December, 1959), 85-98.

7.   Brown, Gerald L., Personal Communication.

8.   Brown, Gregory M., "Psychiatric and Neurological Aspects of Endocrine Disease", <u>Hospital Practice</u>, X (August, 1975), 71-82.

9.   Bryan, W. T. and K. Bryan, "Cytotoxic Reactions in the Diagnosis of Food Allergy", <u>Laryngoscope</u>, LXXIX, (1969), 1453-1472.

10.   Cohen, A. M., Alisan Teitelbaum, Miriam Balogh, and J. J. Groen, "Effect of Interchanging Bread and Sucrose as a Main Source of Carbohydrate in a Low Fat Diet on the Glucose Tolerance Curve of Healthy Volunteer Subjects", <u>American Journal of Clinical Nutrition</u>, XIX (July, 1966), 59-62.

11.   Coleman, Mary "Serotonin and Central Nervous System Syndromes of Childhood: A Review", <u>Journal of Autism and Childhood Schizophrenia</u>, III (1973), 27-35.

12.   Conners, C. K., C. Goyetter, et al., "Food Additives and Hyperkinesis: A controlled Double-Blind Experiment", <u>Pediatrics</u>, LVIII (1976), 154.

13.   Cott, Allen, "A Hyperactive Child Needs Nutrients, Not Drugs", <u>Prevention</u>, XXIII (April, 1971), 169-176.

14. Coulombe, P., J. H. Dussault, and P. Walter, "Plasma Catecholamine Concentration in Hyperthyroidism and Hypothyroidism", <u>Metabolism</u>, XXV (1976), 973.

15. Crawford, I. L. and J. D. Connor, "Zinc and Hippocampal Function", <u>The Journal of Orthomolecular Psychiatry</u>, IV (1975), 39-52.

16. Crook, William G., "Food Allergy—The Great Masquerader", <u>Pediatric Clinics of North America</u>, XXII (February, 1975), 227-238.

17. Daughaday, William H., "Growth Hormone", <u>American Diabetes Association Forecast</u>, XXI (May, 1977), 1-4.

18. Davis, Richard E., "Manic Depressive Variant of Childhood: A Preliminary Report", <u>American Journal of Psychiatry</u>, CXXXVI (May, 1979), 702-706.

19. Duncan, Garfield G., <u>Diseases of Metabolism</u>, Philadelphia, W. B. Saunders Company, 1952.

20. Fernstrom, John D., "Effects of the Diet on Brain Neurotransmitters", <u>Metabolism</u>, XXVI (February, 1977), 207-223.

21. Guyton, Arthur C., <u>Function of the Human Body</u>, Philadelphia, W. B Saunders Company, 1974.

22. Hawkins, David and Linus Pauling, <u>Orthomolecular Psychiatry Treatment of Schizophrenia</u>, San Francisco, W. H. Freeman and Company, 1973.

23. Hoffer, Abram, <u>Schizophrenia</u>, Cleveland, Ohio, Karpat Publishing Company, Inc., 1972.

24. Jennings, Joan, "Diet, Hormones and Diabetes", <u>Prevention</u>, XXIII (December, 1971), 83-97.

25. Kiem, Joe G., James W. Anderson, and Kyleen Ward, "Beneficial Effects of a High Carbohydrate, High Fiber Diet on Hyperglycemic Diabetic Men", <u>The American Journal of Clinical Nutrition</u>, XXIX (August, 1976), 895-899.

26. Leonard, Jon F., J. L. Hofer, and Nathan Pritikin, <u>Live Longer Now</u>, New York, Grosset and Dunlap Publishers, 1974.

27. Levitan, H., "Food, Drug and Cosmetic Dyes: Biological Effects Related to Lipid Solubility", <u>Proceedings of the National Academy of Science</u>, July, 1977.

28. McGeer, Patrick L., Personal Communication.

29. McGeer, Patrick L., "The Chemistry of Mind," <u>American Scientist</u>, LIX (March-April, 1971), 221-229.

30. Nordgren, L., and C. Von Scheele, <u>Acta Medical Scandinavica</u>, CXC (1976), 233.

31. Page, Melvin, "Degeneration Regeneration", St. Petersburg Beach, Florida, <u>Nutritional Development</u>, 1977.

32. Page, Melvin, personal communication.

33. Pfeiffer, Carl C., <u>Mental and Elemental Nutrients</u>, New Canaan, Connecticut, Keats Publishing Company, Inc., 1975.

34. Pfeiffer, Carl C., Jack Ward, Moneim El-Meligi, and Allan Cott, <u>The Schizophrenias, Yours and Mine</u>, New York, The Professional Committee of the Schizophrenia Foundation of New Jersey, 1976.

35. Philpott, W. H. "The Significance of Selected Food and Chemical Stressors in Ecological Hypoglycemia and Hyperglycemia," <u>Journal: International Academy of Metabology, Inc.</u>, (May, 1967) 36-41.

36. Pihl, R. D., and M. Parkes, "Hair Element Content in L.D. Children," <u>Science</u>, CXVIII (October, 1977) 204-206.

37. Powers, Hugh W. S., Personal interview.

38. Proceedings of the 7th International Congress of Nutrition, 1966, Vol. 1-5.

39. Rabinowitch, I. M., "The Effects of High Carbohydrate - Low Calorie Diet upon Carbohydrate Tolerance in Diabetes Mellitus," <u>The Canadian Medical Association Journal</u>, LVIII (August, 1935), 136-144.

40. Ringsdorf, W. M., Jr., M. O. Cheraskin, and R. R. Ramsey, Jr., "Sucrose, Neutrophillic Phagocytosis and Resistance to Disease," <u>Dental Survey</u>, LII (December, 1976), 46-48.

41. Rogers, G. S., <u>Dietary Treatment of Hyperactive Children</u>, unpublished doctoral dissertation College of Arts and Sciences, North Texas State University, Denton, Texas, 1976.

42. Sears, Barry, <u>Enter the Zone</u>, New York City, New York, Harper Collins Publishers, Inc. (Regan Books), 1995.

43. Springer, Ninfa S. and Norma L. Fricke, "Nutrition and Drug Therapy for Persons with Developmental Disabilities," <u>American Journal of Mental Deficiency</u>, LXXX (1975), 317-322.

44. "The Thyroid and the Psychiatrist", (author not given) <u>British Medical Journal</u>, I (April 9, 1977), 931-932.

45. Tintera, John, <u>Hypoadrenocorticism</u>, Adrenal Metabolic Research Society of the Hypoglycemia Foundation, 1 Park Lane, Mount Vernon, New York, 10552.

46. Williams, Rogers, and Dwight K. Kalita, <u>A Physicians Handbook on Orthomolecular Medicine</u>, New York, Pergamon Press, 1977.

47. Wunderlich, Ray C., "The Hyperactivity Complex," <u>Journal of Optometric Vision Development</u>, VIII (March, 1977), 8-45.

48. Wunderlich, Ray C., "Paranoid Schizophrenia as a Manifestation of Metabolic Derangement: Successful Management by Metabolic Therapy," <u>Journal of International Academy of Preventive Medicine</u>, I (September, 1976), 21-36.

Chapter 3

A STUDY OF TWENTY-NINE HYPERACTIVE CHILDREN

In 1979 I conducted a study of hyperactive children for my doctoral dissertation. Taking part in the study were 29 children who had been diagnosed "hyperactive." All of the children received the following tests:

{ 6 Hour Glucose Tolerance Test

{ Cytotoxic Food Test, ACTH,

{ Growth Hormone, Thyroid (T-4), and

{ the Hair Mineral Analysis

The 6 Hour Glucose Tolerance Tests and the Hair Mineral Analysis were performed by Southwest Medical Laboratories, Inc., 1111 W. Mockingbird Lane, Suite 1320, Dallas, TX 75247. HEW 42-1069, Medicare Number 45-8312

The Cytotoxic Allergy Invitro Test was performed by Broadway Medical Lab, Inc., 3232 Broadway, Garland, TX 75041. HEW Medicare Lab Lic. # 45-8333.

ACTH, Growth Hormone, and T-4 Thyroxine were performed by Nichols Institute, 1300 S. Beacon St., San Pedro, California, 90731, Federal Interstate License 04-1124.

The children were divided into two groups with 17 in the Experimental Group and 12 in the Comparison (i.e., control) Group. The Experimental Group did not eat sugar or junk food. They ate nutritious food and took nutritional supplements daily. The Comparison Group got no treatment, but their parents received group Parent Effectiveness Training or PET.

The children in the Experimental Group showed the most improvement, as they lost 53% of their symptoms in twelve weeks. The Comparison Group improved, as well, and they lost 34% of their symptoms during the same period of time.

The test results follow.

DR. SHIRLEY LACY

MEDICAL TEST DATA FOR EXPERIMENTAL GROUP*

Subject	Hypo-glycemia	Pre-Diabetes	Food Allergy	T-4 Normal	T-4 Abnormal	ACTH L	ACTH N	ACTH H	GROWTH L	GROWTH N	GROWTH H	Calcium L	Calcium N	Calcium H	Magnesium L	Magnesium N	Magnesium H
1		X	34		12.7		71.2				8.6			60		2.5	
2		X	18	8.5			61.5			<1.0			20		0.5		
3	X		13	10			60.4			<1.0			52		1.5		
4	X		16	6			42.2			<1.0			31		0.8		
5		X	12	9.9				149			29		55		1.5		
6		X	8	9.5			42.1			1.8		26			1.4		
7	X		15	10			30.2			<1.0			39		0.6		
8	X		14	8.2			52.1			<1.0		10			0.3		
9		X	15	8			36.8			<1.0			44		1.4		
10		X	19	6.3			28.6			17				100	1.9		
11		X	15	8.1			35.2			11			49		1.2		
12	X		18	9.1			38.6			1.6			86		3.1		
13		X	24	8.1				162		1.3				116	3.7		
14	X		17	9.9			62.6			<1.0				165		3.2	
15		X	19	9.2			36.3			4				126		2.5	
16	X		14	7.4			54.8			<1.0				58		3.6	
17	X		17	5.8			43.7			14			61		1.8		

*T-4 in mcg. Per dl., ACTH in pg. per ml., Growth Hormone in ng. per ml., Hair Analysis in mg. % (in 100 grams of hair);

Normal limits were those specified by each laboratory.

Six Hour Glucose Tolerance Test, Hair Analysis completed at Southwest Medical Laboratory, Cytotoxic Food Test completed at Broadway Medical Laboratory, and T-4, ACTH, Growth Hormone done at Nichols Institute.

24

MEDICAL TEST DATA FOR EXPERIMENTAL GROUP

Subject	Sodium			Potassium			Copper			Zinc			Phosphorus			Iron		
	L	N	H	L	N	H	L	N	H	L	N	H	L	N	H	L	N	H
1			6.1		0.7			1.4		12				12				7.4
2		3			0.6			0.9		5			8				0.8	
3		1.7			1.5			2.2		2			6					3.1
4		1.1		0.3					7.5	6				13				2.4
5		0.7		0.3					6.7	7				10				3.4
6		1.5			0.5			3.1		12				10				3.9
7		1.6			0.6				5.5	6				11				2.5
8		1.2		0.1					3.6	4				12				3.1
9		1.3			1.4				13.6	5				10				4.5
10		1.5			0.8				15.1	7				11				4.4
11		2.3			1.5				24.5	5			8					4.8
12		2.6			2.6			3.8		6			8					2.7
13		1.5			1.2			3.9		7				10		<0.1		
14		1.0			0.9				8.4		14			12				6.6
15		2.1			3.8				21.9	7				12			1.9	
16		1.5			0.7			1.7		9				10				6.6
17		5			1.1			4.7		9				14			5.7	

DR. SHIRLEY LACY

MEDICAL TEST DATA FOR EXPERIMENTAL GROUP

Subject	Manganese			Chromium			Lithium			Cadmium			Lead		
	L	N	H	L	N	H	L	N	H	L	N	H	L	N	H
1		0.12			0.02			<.01			0.04		0.3		
2		0.11		<.01				<.01			0.08			1.2	
3		0.1			0.04			<.01			0.1			1.3	
4		0.09			0.05			<.01				0.17			1.9
5		0.11				0.23		<.01				0.3			
6		0.04			0.09			<.01			0.1			1.2	
7		0.05			0.07			<.01			0.08			0.9	
8		0.02			0.01			<.01			0.04			0.5	
9		0.09			0.07			<.01			0.12				1.9
10		0.07			0.52			<.01			0.14				3.1
11		0.10				0.12		<.01			0.12				4.2
12		0.12		<.01				<.01				0.27		0.6	
13		0.08		<.01				<.01			0.14			0.4	
14			0.19					<.01				0.25			2.2
15		0.7			0.09			<.01				0.24			1.7
16			0.24		0.06			<.01				0.85			1.8
17		0.09			0.1			<.01			0.13			1.1	

MEDICAL TEST DATA FOR COMPARISON GROUP*

Subject	Hypo-glycemia	Pre-Diabetes	Food Allergy	T-4 Normal	T-4 Abnormal	ACTH L	ACTH N	ACTH H	GROWTH L	GROWTH N	GROWTH H	Calcium L	Calcium N	Calcium H	Magnesium L	Magnesium N	Magnesium H
18	X		17	6.8			42.2			<1.0		13			0.5		
19	X		16	11			67.5			<1.0			43		0.9		
20		X	17	7.8			28.4			<1.0		1.7				3.5	
21		X	18	5.9						<1.0				129		5.9	
22		X	23	6.3			35.2			<1.0			28		0.3		
23		X	19	9.6				106		1.3			54		0.9		
24	X		16		4.9		42.8			<1.0				94		4.4	
25		X	14	8.7				130		<1.0			78		4.3		
26		X	18	8.3			86.1			1.4			40		0.7		
27		X	19	7.9			38.6			2.8				119	1.7		
28	X		11	5.3			71.4			2.6				164	2.3		
29		X		4.6			57.3			<1.0				85	1.5		

*T-4 in mcg. per dl., ACTH in pg. per ml., Growth Hormone in ng. per ml., Hair Analysis in mg.% (in 100 grams of hair).

Normal limites were those specified by each laboratory.

Six Hour Glucose Tolerance Test, Hair Analysis completed at Southwest Medical Laboratory,

Cytotoxic Food Test completed at Broadway Medical Laboratory, and T-4, ACTH, Growth Hormone done at Nichols Institute.

27

MEDICAL TEST DATA FOR COMPARISON GROUP - Continued

Subject	Sodium			Potassium			Copper			Zinc			Phosphorus			Iron		
	L	N	H	L	N	H	L	N	H	L	N	H	L	N	H	L	N	H
18	0.4				0.7			2.8		5				14				3.1
19		2.6			2.6			4.8		5				10				3.7
20		1.2			1.7			3.2		7				11				7.7
21		1.6		0.2				2				22		10			1.2	
22	0.1			0.1				1.3		6				13			1.2	
23		1.5			0.6			1.1		11			6			<0.1		
24		0.7			0.8				13.7	5				10		0.2		
25		1.2			0.5			3.2		10				10				3.2
26		2.3			0.7			1.2		12					19			4
27		2.4			0.7			2		12			7					2.5
28	0.4			0.4				3.2		11			6			<0.1		
29		2		0.4					5.3	6			7			<0.1		

MEDICAL TEST DATA FOR COMPARISON GROUP

Subject	Manganese			Chromium			Lithium			Cadmium			Lead		
	L	N	H	L	N	H	L	N	H	L	N	H	L	N	H
18	0.07				0.09			0.01			0.16				2.1
19	0.09				0.01			0.01			0.16				2.2
20	<.01			<.01				<.01			0.13			0.8	
21			0.2		0.1			0.01			0.12			0.7	
22		0.04			0.05			<.01			0.05			0.7	
23		0.06		<.01				<.01				0.29		1.2	
24		0.05		<.01				0.01			0.05			1.1	
25		0.1			0.03			<.01			0.09			1.4	
26		0.02		<.01				<.01			0.06		0.3		
27		0.08		<.01				<.01			0.06		0.3		
28		0.06		<.01				<.01			0.14			1.0	
29		0.08		<.01				<.01				0.24			1.6

TABLE XXV

ALLERGIC FOODS FOR SUBJECTS IN EXPERIMENTAL GROUP

1. milk	11. rye	21. pork	31. celery	41. tuna	51. pineapple
2. beef	12. turkey	22. green peas	32. cucumber	42. shrimp	52. lamb
3. soybean	13. orange	23. pinto beans	33. cabbage	43. cod	53. coconut
4. corn	14. beet sugar	24. carrots	34. coffee	44. ocean perch	54. almonds
5. bakers yeast	15. cane sugar	25. peach	35. tea	45. red snapper	55. plum
6. egg	16. chocolate	26. grape, concord	36. onion	46. peanut	56. pear
7. wheat	17. tomato	27. green beans	37. black pepper	47. walnut	57. apricot
8. cottonseed	18. cottonseed	28. lettuce	38. garlic	48. pecan	58. strawberry
9. chicken	19. malt	29. grapefruit	39. brewers yeast	49. apple	59. mushroom
10. oats	20. Irish potato	30. lemon	40. salmon	50. banana	60. olive

Subject:

1. 1 3 4 8 9 11 13 16 17 18 19 21 22 23 25 26 33 38 39 40 41 42 43 44 45 46 47 48 49 50 53 54 59 60
2. 5 8 10 15 18 19 24 26 33 36 38 39 42 43 48 51 54 60
3. 1 4 9 13 16 21 27 33 42 48 54 57 60
4. 1 8 12 18 25 29 30 31 34 38 39 42 45 48 51 59
5. 1 4 7 16 19 22 27 33 42 48 50 54
6. 5 16 20 22 29 39 48 58
7. 5 6 7 12 16 18 21 27 33 36 42 48 51 54 58
8. 1 4 5 6 8 9 16 30 31 34 42 47 48 57
9. 4 5 7 10 16 21 22 38 42 46 48 54 57 58 59
10. 1 4 5 8 11 16 21 24 28 33 35 37 41 42 47 48 50 53 54 58
11. 1 4 5 8 20 22 25 33 36 39 42 48 52 59 60
12. 13 16 17 21 22 26 27 28 31 32 33 34 39 42 48 52 58
13. 4 5 7 8 9 10 11 13 18 19 20 21 32 39 42 45 48 49 50 51 54 58 59 60
14. 1 2 3 5 9 11 16 19 20 28 31 32 33 42 47 54 57
15. 1 4 5 7 8 10 11 12 16 19 26 34 39 42 43 46 48 57 58
16. 1 4 8 16 19 22 23 27 38 42 46 51 55 58
17. 1 2 3 4 5 7 13 19 22 23 25 30 36 39 42 48 49

TABLE XXVI

ALLERGIC FOODS FOR SUBJECTS IN COMPARISON GROUP

1 milk	11 rye	21 pork	31 celery	41 tuna	51 pineapple
2 beef	12 turkey	22 green peas	32 cucumber	42 shrimp	52 lamb
3 soybean	13 orange	23 pinto beans	33 cabbage	43 cod	53 coconut
4 corn	14 beet sugar	24 carrots	34 coffee	44 ocean perch	54 almonds
5 bakers yeast	15 cane sugar	25 peach	35 tea	45 red snapper	55 plum
6 egg	16 chocolate	26 grape, concord	36 onion	46 peanut	56 pear
7 wheat	17 tomato	27 green beans	37 black pepper	47 walnut	57 apricot
8 rice	18 cottonseed	28 lettuce	38 garlic	48 pecan	58 strawberry
9 chicken	19 malt	29 grapefruit	39 brewers yeast	49 apple	59 mushroom
10 oats	20 Irish potato	30 lemon	40 salmon	50 banana	60 olive

Subject

18. 1 2 3 4 5 8 11 18 19 23 26 32 34 42 48 54 57
19. 4 5 8 13 17 18 22 25 28 35 36 37 38 48 53 56
20. 1 5 12 13 17 18 21 26 29 33 37 41 42 48 54 57 60
21. 1 2 4 6 7 8 10 13 21 33 34 40 42 45 46 47 48 54
22. 1 4 8 10 11 17 18 20 22 29 32 33 39 40 42 43 44 47 48 49 54 56 60
23. 1 4 5 12 16 19 21 22 23 26 28 32 39 42 48 51 54 57 58
24. 1 4 9 12 15 16 29 33 35 39 42 43 48 51 54 59
25. 1 4 7 10 13 16 22 27 42 43 46 47 48 57
26. 1 2 4 5 7 11 16 19 28 40 41 42 43 44 45 48 54 57
27. 1 4 7 11 14 16 17 20 24 27 32 35 39 46 47 49 54 55 60
28. 1 4 7 10 18 21 28 34 35 39 42 46 47 48 50 54 57 60
29. 4 5 6 7 12 16 21 24 33 34 37 48 50 51 54 55

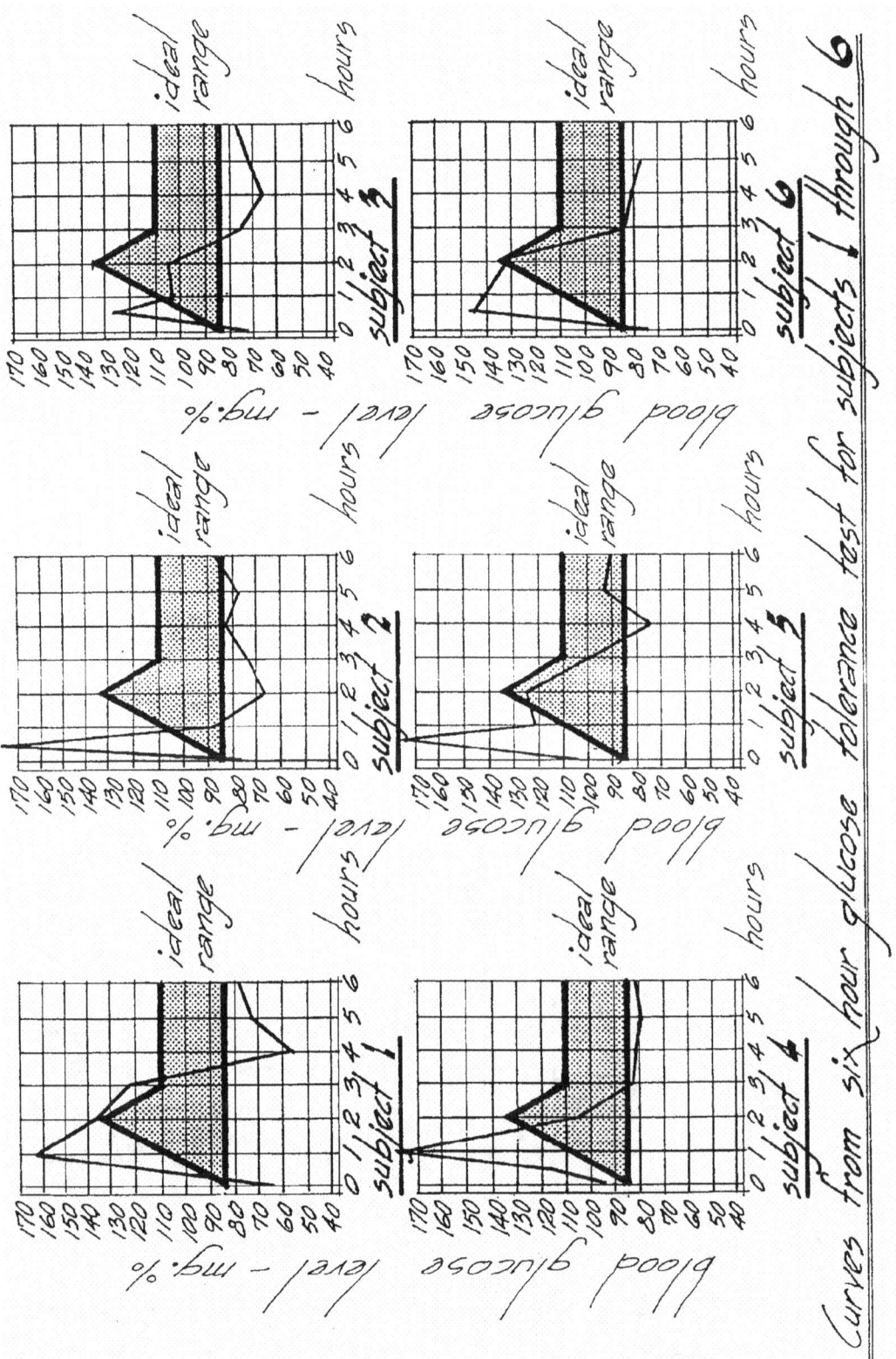

Curves from six hour glucose tolerance test for subjects 1 through 6

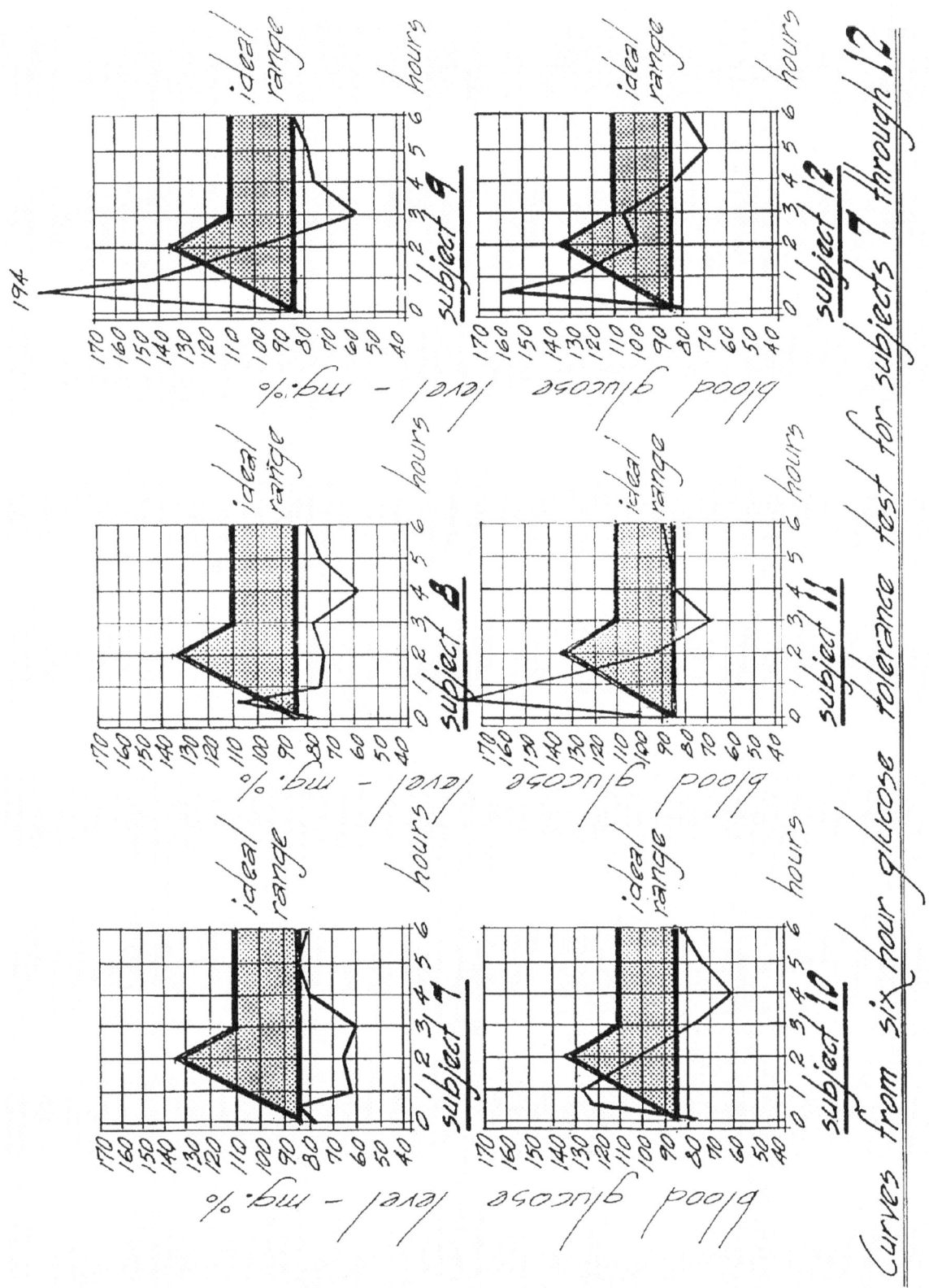

Curves from six hour glucose tolerance test for subjects 7 through 12

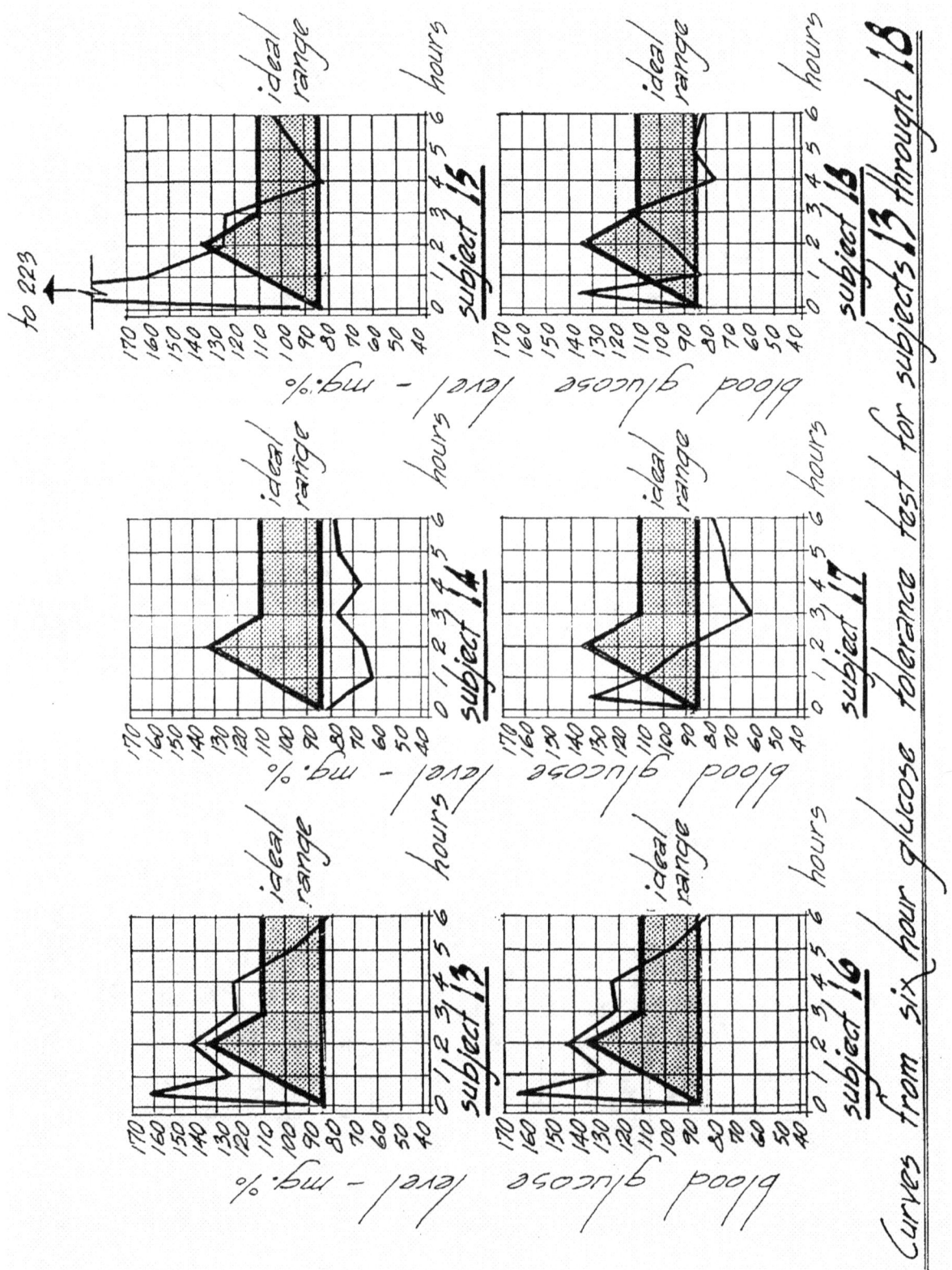

Curves from six hour glucose tolerance test for subjects 13 through 18

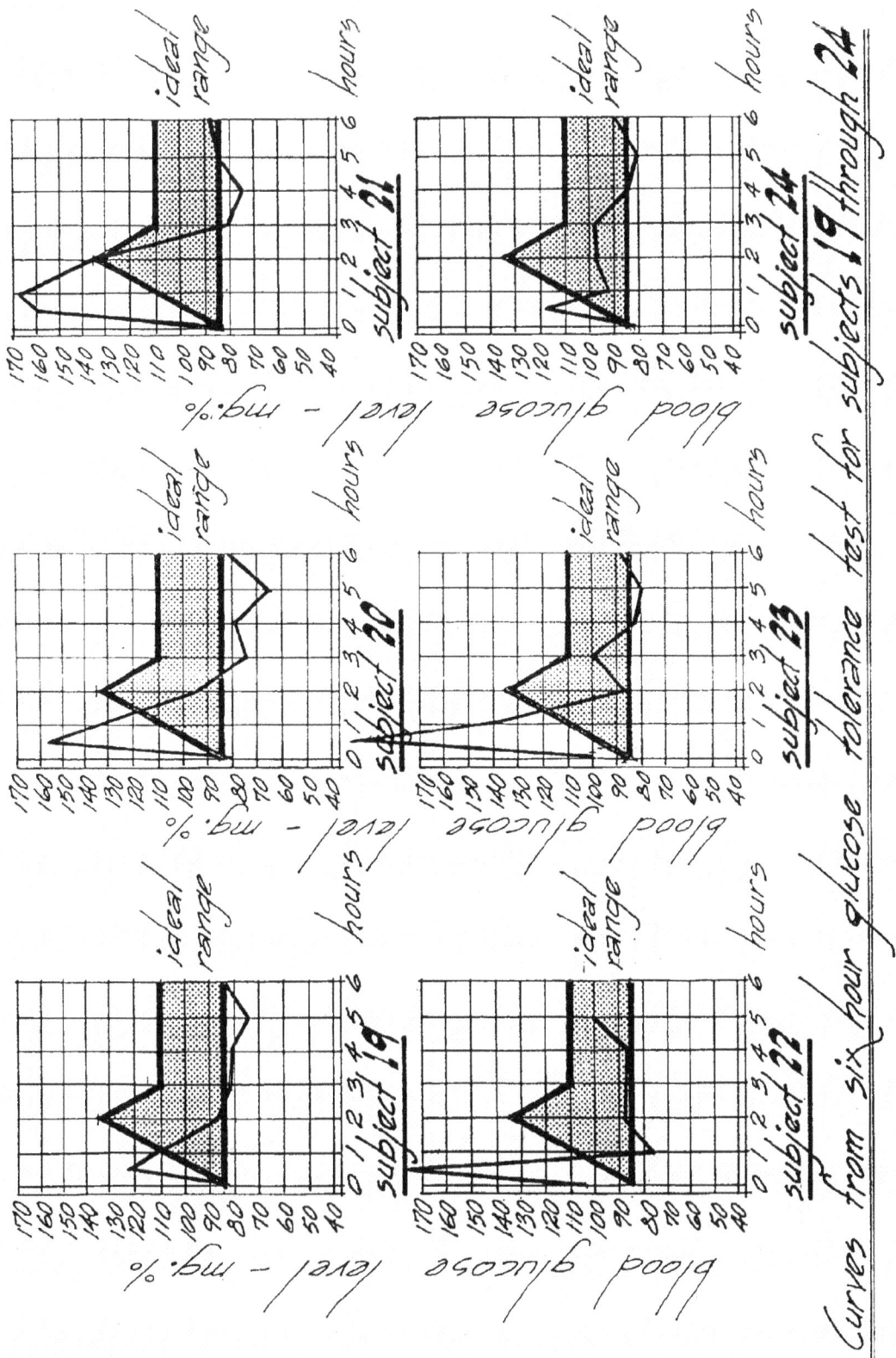

Curves from six hour glucose tolerance test for subjects 19 through 24

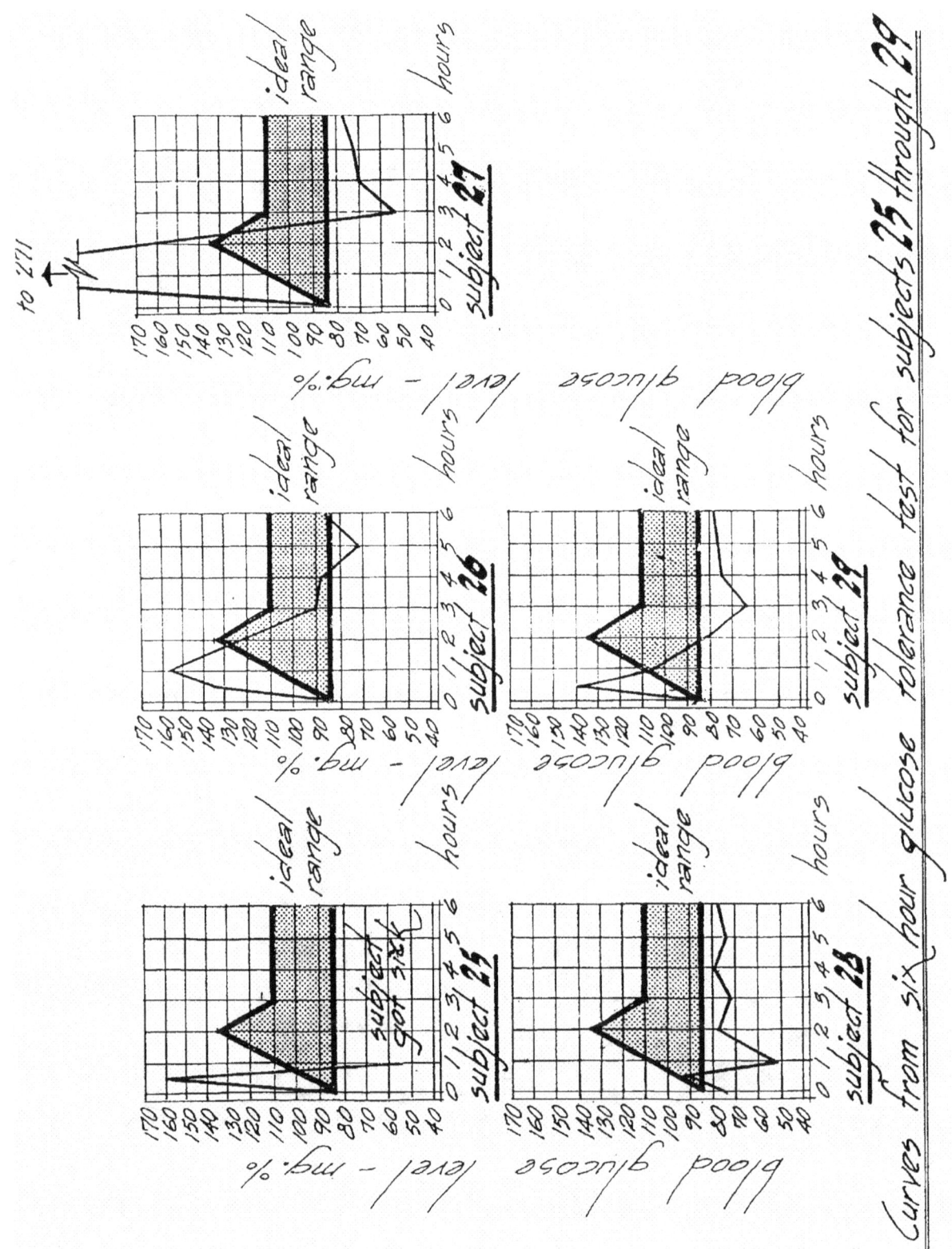

Curves from six hour glucose tolerance test for subjects 25 through 29

TEST RESULTS
FOR 29 HYPERACTIVE CHILDREN

Six Hour Glucose Tolerance Test (hypoglycemic or Pre-Diabetic)
29 = 100%

	Low		Normal		High	
	No.	%	No.	%	No.	%
ACTH	0	0	24	85.7	4	14.3
Growth	0	0	27	93.0	2	7.0
Thyroid (T-4)	0	0	28	96.6	1	3.4

Reaction to CytoToxic Food Test
(Reaction of White Cells to Foods) 29 = 100%

	Low		Normal		High	
	No.	%	No.	%	No.	%
Minerals taken from the Hair Mineral Analysis						
Calcium	4	13.7	14	48.2	11	37.9
Magnesium	22	76	7	24.1	0	0.0
Manganese	3	10.3	23	79.3	3	10.3
Chromium	10	34.5	17	58.6	2	7.0
Lithium	0	0	29	100	0	0.0
Cadmium	0.0	0.0	21	72.4	8	27.5
Lead	3	10.3	15	51.7	10	34.4
Sodium	3	10.3	25	86.2	1	3.4
Potassium	7	24.1	22	75.8	0	0
Copper	0.0	0.0	18	62.0	11	37.9
Zinc	27	93.1	1	3.4	1	3.4
Phosphorus	8	27.5	20	69.0	1	3.4
Iron	5	17.2	5	17.2	19	65.6

Fig. 3—Disorders found in families of hyperkinetic children

ALCOHOLISM	HYPOGLYCEMIA	DIABETES	DYSLEXIA	DEPRESSION	SCHIZOPHRENIA	OBESITY	STROKE	THYROID	ALLERGIES
		*		*	*	*			
*	*	*				*		*	
*		*						*	
*		*						*	*
*	*	*		*	*		*		
*		*			*	*	*		
*		*					*		
*			*						
*		*		****					
	*			*	*				
*	*	*		*	*				
					*				
ADOPTED **							*		
	*	*					*		
	*			**			*		*

38

Chapter 4

Medical Test Findings

The demographic and statistical data of this study show that the subjects in the experimental group ranged in age from five to seventeen and had from eleven to twenty-nine symptoms listed on the Conners Parent Questionnaire. The subjects in the comparison group ranged in age from six to sixteen and had from eleven to twenty-five symptoms listed on the Conners Parent Questionnaire (see page 86). Both treatments resulted in a reduction of all symptoms except enuresis for children in the experimental and control groups.

The medical test data, however, also yielded additional information, which warrants consideration in discussion of hyperkinetic children. Biochemical abnormalities were found in children in both groups (see p. 24-32 and p. 38.).

The curves from the six-hour glucose tolerance test (see p. 33-37) range from flat and hypoglycemic curves to pre-diabetic curves. Some curves were bimodal. Steep drops in blood sugar, as exhibited by glucose tolerance curves, were seen in conjunction with the symptoms of headache, drowsiness, sleep, loss of color vision, blurred vision, and temper tantrums. Blood sugars considerably below the normal range were examples of excessive insulin production.

Many food allergies were found in these children. According to information obtained from the laboratory, one might expect to find at least five food allergies in the normal person. These children had between eight and thirty-four, according to the cyto-toxic food test. To determine the allergic food, the lab technician observed the child's blood placed on a pre-prepared slide containing a food sample. If a food killed all of the white cells in the blood, then that food was called an "allergic food" and it was eliminated from the diet. Sixty foods were tested in this manner. Twenty-two out of twenty-nine children reacted to cow's milk.

Out of twenty-nine children, one was found to have low thyroid. He was given thyroid supplements by his physician.

Four abnormally high ACTH values were found. The head of the Endocrinology Department at a large teaching hospital did not feel that the values were high enough to indicate the presence of a tumor, so the children were not treated for this abnormality.

The secretion of growth hormone was abnormally high in two children. Two endocrinologists who were consulted did not know the meaning of this abnormality. Both endocrinologists felt that sixteen growth hormone readings of <1 indicated an abnormally large part in a sample of twenty-nine children. Pfeiffer [20] relates a study where dwarfs who were given 100 mg. of zinc sulphate supplements and a balanced diet grew 10.5 centimeters in height. It is possible, then, that the presence of zinc is necessary for the release of growth hormone. As already stated, eating sugar and raising the sugar level in the blood causes a cessation of the secretion of growth hormone [11]. According to the parents, all of the children tested ate and enjoyed sugar foods and drinks. Bivens, Lebovitz, and Feldman found that the administration of Cyproheptadine, a serotonin antagonist, resulted in a 59 percent reduction ($p < 0.01$) in plasma growth hormone. Their study lends support to the contention that serotonin is one of the factors that causes growth hormone secretion [2]. Since hyperkinetic children have been found to be low in serotonin [8] perhaps this explains the large incidence of low growth hormone. A reduction in growth hormone would cause an increased allergic reaction to foods because of the reduction in enzymes which break up the food [13]. The serotonin level can be raised with B6, beCALM'd, 30 minutes of daily sunlight without glasses, exercise, Vitamin C, 5 HTP, hydration and fish oil.

Fifteen children had abnormal calcium levels, eleven were high, and four were low. The calcium-phosphorus ratio has long been emphasized as being necessary for healthy tissue. Adequate calcium levels are essential for healthy blood and bones. Calcium eases insomnia, and it helps to regulate the heartbeat. It plays a part in muscle growth, muscle contraction, and the transmission of nerve impulses. Calcium aids in the body's utilization of iron and helps to activate enzymes (catalysts important for metabolism). The effectiveness of calcium is diminished by lack of hydrochloric acid, magnesium, and vitamin D. The eating of fat or chocolate as well as the lack of exercise and excessive stress all interfere with the absorption of calcium [18]. Pfeiffer has stated that hypoglycemics on a high protein diet experience urinary calcium loss because of the acid ash of the protein and they need to take dolomitic calcium tablets twice a day. High calcium has been found in patients with psychiatric depression and the depression lifts as the blood serum calcium is lowered. In addition, he states that patients whose depression is lifted by lithium therapy show a decrease of calcium and magnesium in the blood serum and an increase in urinary excretion of these two elements [20].

Out of the twenty-nine children tested, twenty-two of them were low in magnesium and seven children had magnesium levels in the normal range.

Magnesium activates enzymes necessary for the metabolism of carbohydrates and amino acids. It plays a role in neuromuscular contractions and helps to regulate the acid-alkaline balance in the body. Magnesium promotes the absorption of calcium, phosphorus, sodium and potassium. It helps to utilize B complex and vitamins C and E in the body. Sufficient amounts of magnesium are required in the conversion of blood sugar into energy. Magnesium is also associated with the regulation of body temperature. Many hyperactive children sweat profusely, especially during sleep. Perhaps low levels of magnesium are related to this symptom. Magnesium deficiency can occur in patients with diabetes, alcoholism, kidney malfunction, or those on a high carbohydrate diet. Symptoms of magnesium deficiency may include nervousness, muscle twitch, tremors, tantrums, confusion, and disorientation. The way to eliminate magnesium deficiency is to take dietary supplements and reduce milk consumption, as synthetic vitamin D found in milk binds with magnesium carrying it out of the body [18].

Three children were found to be low in sodium and one was found to be high in sodium. Excess sodium can cause potassium to be lost in the urine, abnormal fluid retention, and high blood pressure. It can be corrected by eliminating table salt. Deficiencies of sodium can cause intestinal gas, weight loss, vomiting, and muscle shrinkage. The conversion of carbohydrates into fat in the digestive process is impaired when sodium is absent. Sodium may be beneficial in eliminating leg cramps, adrenal exhaustion, and diarrhea[18], which are symptoms found in some hyperactive children.

Seven children were found to be low in potassium. Potassium deficiency can result from an excessive intake of salt and refined sugar or from an inadequate intake of fruit and vegetables. A potassium deficiency can cause nervous disorders, insomnia, constipation, slow heart beat, impaired glucose metabolism, weakness, and impairment of neuromuscular function. Diabetics are often found to be deficient in potassium. Potassium can be beneficial in the treatment of diabetes, mononucleosis, diarrhea, insomnia, headache, constipation, impaired muscle activity, and allergies [18]. These conditions are experienced by many hyperactive children.

Eleven children had high copper stores in the hair. According to Pfeiffer [20], high copper is found in people who experience severe anemia, heart attack, depression, mental illness, and death. Copper is a stimulant to the brain, Pfeiffer feels that copper may be a factor related to hyperactivity and autism. Pfeiffer has postulated that high copper and iron and/or zinc and manganese deficiency are primary factors in one type of schizophrenia, histapenia (low histamine). He has stated that histapenic children are hyperactive. In rat studies where brain copper was increased by 36 per cent in a six week period the activity of a zinc containing enzyme, lactic acid dehydrogenase, was decreased. During this period the turnover of serotonin was reduced. Therefore, the low levels of serotonin found in some hyperactive children may be partially caused by high levels of copper. Surplus copper can be ingested in vitamin pills containing copper and in water flowing through copper pipes. Copper is also elevated during an infection or inflammatory state. Zinc plus manganese in dietary doses is effective in increasing copper elimination and reducing copper to normal levels.

Twenty-seven children were found to have low zinc. Zinc is an essential trace mineral having many functions in the body. Zinc is necessary for the absorption and action of vitamins, especially the B complex. It is a constituent of twenty-five enzymes involved in digestion and metabolism. Zinc is a component of insulin. It is essential for general growth and proper development of the reproductive organs. Zinc is stored in parts of the eyes (especially the retina), prostate gland and spermatozoa, skin, hair, fingernails and toenails, and it is present in the white blood cells. Zinc deficiency is associated with fatigue, susceptibility to infection, decreased alertness, loss of taste, poor appetite, loss of vision [20], suboptimal growth, and diabetes [18]. Low levels of zinc in the soil, food processing, careless cooking and the consumption of junk foods contribute to a suboptimal level of zinc in man [20]. Some researchers believe that the ingestion of granulated cane sugar interferes with the absorption of zinc in the body [7,21].

Eight children had low phosphorus. Phosphorus is a very important mineral as it is present in every cell in the body, and a proper balance of calcium and phosphorus is needed for these minerals to be effectively used in the body. Phosphorus plays a part in almost every chemical reaction in the body. It is important for the utilization of carbohydrates, fats, and protein for growth, maintenance and repair of cells and also for the production of energy. Phosphorus is necessary for proper skeletal growth, tooth development, kidney functioning, and transference of nerve impulses. A deficiency of phosphorus can cause lack of appetite, weight loss, or weight gain. Tooth and gum disorders, irregular breathing, mental and physical fatigue, and nervous disorders may arise as a result of a lack of phosphorus. Hyperactive children experience some of these symptoms. The hyperactive child often has disturbed carbohydrate metabolism. He eats white sugar with regularity and this substance impairs metabolism further as well as disturbing the calcium-phosphorus balance. Some children eat diets high in fat and this increases absorption of phosphorus while decreasing the absorption of calcium, thereby upsetting the calcium-phosphorus balance [18].

Five of the children tested were low in iron and nineteen were high in iron. Iron is a mineral concentrate found in the blood and in every cell. The major function of iron is to combine with protein and copper in making hemoglobin, the coloring matter of red blood cells. Hemoglobin transports oxygen in the blood to the tissues. Thus, iron builds up blood and increases resistance to stress and disease. Iron is present in enzymes which promote protein metabolism, and it works with other nutrients to improve respiratory action. Ascorbic acid enhances absorption of iron and vitamin E aids in assimilation of iron. Excess phosphorus, lack of hydrochloric acid, and high intake of cellulose, coffee, and tea interfere with the absorption of iron. Lack of iron reduces the oxygen carrying capacity of the blood, resulting in pale skin, abnormal fatigue, constipation, and difficult breathing. Excessive deposits of iron in the liver and spleen in certain individuals may result from conditions such as cirrhosis of the liver, diabetes or pancreatic insufficiency [18]. Excessive iron can accumulate by drinking from iron vessels or taking vitamins containing iron. High levels of iron can result in headache, shortness of breath, fatigue, dizziness, loss of weight, arthritis, and damage to the liver, pancreas, lungs, and heart. High levels of iron can be fatal [20].

Six children had abnormal levels of manganese, three were low and three were high. Manganese plays a role in activating numerous enzymes. Manganese aids in the utilization of choline, and it activates enzymes that are necessary for utilization of biotin, thiamin, and ascorbic acid. Manganese is necessary for normal skeletal development. It helps maintain sex hormone production, it is important for the formation of blood, and it helps nourish the nerves and brain. A deficiency of manganese can effect glucose tolerance, resulting in the inability to remove excess sugar from the blood by oxidation and storage. Excessive levels of manganese result in reduced absorption of iron. High tissue manganese causes weakness, psychological changes, and motor impairment. It is toxic at high levels.

Ten children were found to be low in chromium and two were found to be high. Chromium stimulates the activity of enzymes involved in the metabolism of glucose for energy and the synthesis of cholesterol and fatty acids. Chromium transports protein in the blood and increases the effectiveness of insulin, facilitating the transport of glucose into the cell. It may also be involved in the synthesis of protein through its binding action with RNA molecules. A deficiency of chromium may be a factor that will upset the function of insulin resulting in depressed growth and severe glucose intolerance in diabetics. Chromium has been found to be beneficial in the treatment of diabetes.

Twenty-five lithium levels were found to be below detectable levels. Twenty-two parents and grandparents of children in the experimental group suffered from alcoholism, depression, and schizophrenia, disorders which have been effectively treated with lithium. Projecting into the future, these children may develop such disorders if chemical balancing is not achieved before they become adults. Lithium has been used to reduce symptoms in schizophrenics [1], to eliminate aggressive behavior [15], and to improve symptoms such as overactivity, lack of concentration, difficulty reading, tantrums, and bed wetting in the hyperactive child [5]. Some manic depressive patients have an inherited disorder of lithium transport in erythrocytes which causes their low lithium [19]. The effects produced by the administration of lithium chloride are the increase of brain glucose, brain lactate, and brain glycogen in rats [22], the increase in serum calcium and magnesium followed by lifting of depression and urinary excretion of these two elements [20]. Also reported was the increase in hemoglobin, platelet count, and white cell count in humans [3] and the increase in tryptophan uptake in striate synaptosomes as well as increased conversion of tryptophan to serotonin in rats [16]. Since hyperactive children have been found to be low in serotonin [8], it appears that the serotonin level and the growth hormone level could both be elevated by administering adequate amounts of lithium. This would increase the amount of enzymes [13] as well as white cells [3], thereby reducing the allergic reaction to food.

Eight children showed high cadmium levels. Cadmium is a toxic trace mineral with no biological function in humans. Forty per cent more cadmium is found in the urine of hypertensive patients than in the urine of normotensive persons [18]. It is stored in the body in place of zinc when the proportion between the two is unfavorably out of balance. Zinc is a natural antagonist to cadmium, and its toxic effects can be kept under control in the body by the presence of zinc. Since most of the children were low in zinc, dietary supplements should reduce the cadmium levels. Cadmium is found in refined flour, rice, and sugar as well as coffee and tea. Therefore, reduced intake of these foods should also contribute to reduced cadmium levels [18].

Lead levels in the hyperactive children studied were found to be abnormally low in three children and high in ten children. High lead is known to be associated with hyperactivity and mental retardation [20]. Sources of lead include dirt, paint, paper, soft water flowing through lead pipes, cigarette smoking, seams of fruit juice cans, pork, beef, and turkey liver as well as exhaust from automobiles. Other methods of taking in excessive lead include living downwind from a zinc smelter, eating plants grown by the side of the road or eating animals that feed alongside of the road. The way to reduce lead is to remove it from the immediate environment, to take a chelating agent such as penicillamine, and to eat a diet high in calcium as calcium protects body tissues from lead contamination [20].

What we have learned from these tests is that there are many biochemical imbalances found in hyperactive children. These imbalances may be caused by heredity, a polluted environment, and food and water that is deficient in necessary minerals thereby causing a deficiency of enzymes and inability to break up food. Important also are ineffective habits which include lack of sunlight and exercise, the use of drugs, the habitual eating of refined flour, rice, and sugar, fatty foods, chocolate, coffee and tea and the preference for canned foods over fresh ones. The treatment for some hyperactive children appears to be identifying imbalances, changing habits, and nutrient intake. In addition, it is important to clean up the environment, avoid allergic foods, and take hypoallergenic multi-vitamins and specially formulated vitamin, mineral, amino acid supplements called "beCALM'd", as well as fish oil.

Chapter Bibliography

1. Alexander, Paul E., Daniel P Van Kammen, and William E. Bunney, Jr., "Antipsychotic Effects of Lithium in Schizophrenia", American Journal of Psychiatry, CXXXVI (March, 1979), 283-286.

2. Bivens, Carl H., Harold E. Lebovitz, and Jerome M. Feldman, "Inhibition of Hypoglycemia-Induced Growth Hormone Secretion by the Serotonin Antagonists Cyproheptadine and Methysergide", The New England Journal of Medicine, CCLXXXIX (August, 197 3), 236-239.

3. Blum, Stuart F., "Lithium Therapy of Aplastic Anemia", New England Journal of Medicine, CCC (March, 1979), 677.

4. Bottenberg, Robert A. and Joe H. Ward, Jr., U.S. Department of Commerce, National Bureau of Standards Institute for Applied Technology, Technical Documentary Report PRL-TOR-63-6, March, 1963, pp. 86-88.

5. Bowdan, Newton D., "Hyperactivity or Affective Illness", American Journal of Psychiatry, CXXXIV (March, 1977), 329

6. Breneman, James C., "Allergic Cystitis: The Cause of Nocturnal Enuresis", General Practitioner, XX (December, 1959), 85-98.

7. Cheraskin, E., Telephone conversation.

8. Coleman, Mary, "Serotonin and Central Nervous System Syndromes of Childhood: A Review", Journal of Autism and Childhood Schizophrenia, III (1973), 27-35.

9. Cott, A. Allen, "A Hyperactive Child Needs Nutrients, Not Drugs", Prevention, XXIII (April, 1971), 169-176.

10. Crook, William G., "Food Allergy—the Great Masquerader", Pediatric Clinics of North America, XXII (February, 1975), 227-238.

11. Daughaday, William H., "Growth Hormone", ADA Forecast, XXI (November-December, 1968), 1-4.

12. Duncan, Garfield G., Diseases of Metabolism, Philadelphia, W. B. Sanders Company. 1952

13. Guyton, Arthur C., Function of the Human Body, Philadelphia, W. B. Saunders Company, 1974.

14. Hoffer, Abram, <u>Schizophrenia</u>, Cleveland Ohio, Karpat Publishing Company, Inc., 1972.

15. Kerr, W. C., "Lithium Salts in the Management of a Child Batterer", <u>The Medical Journal of Australia</u>, II, Part 2(September 11, 1976). 414-415.

16. Lanoir, J. And D. Lardennois, "The Action of Lithium Carbonate on the Sleep-Waking Cycle in the Cat", <u>Electronencephalography and Clinical Neurophysiology</u>, XLII (1977), 676-690.

17. McGeer, Patrick L., "The Chemistry of Mind," <u>American Scientist</u>, LIX (March-April, 1971), 221-229.

18. <u>Minerals for Nutrition</u>, Computer Laboratory Services, Inc., P.O. Box 2627, Richardson, Texas 75080.

19. Ostrow, David G., Gyanshyam N. Pandy, John M. Davis, Stephen W. Hurt, and M.D. Tosteson, "A Heritable Disorder of Lithium Transport in Erythrocytes of a Subpopulation of Manic-Depressive Patients", <u>American Journal of Psychiatry</u>, CXXXV (September, 1978), 1070-1078.

20. Pfeiffer, Carl C., <u>Mental and Elemental Nutrients</u>, New Canaan, Connecticut, Keats Publishing, Inc., 1975.

21. Pfeiffer, Carl C., Personal communication.

22. Plenge, P., "Acute Lithium Effects on Rat Brain Glucose Metabolism—in vivo", <u>International Pharmaco-psychiatry</u>, II (1976), 84-92.

23. Powers, Hugh W. S., Personal interview in Dallas, Texas.

24. Randolph, Theron G., "Allergy as a Causative Factor of Fatigue, Irritability, and Behavior Problems of Children", <u>Journal of Pediatrics</u>, XXXI (July-December, 1947), 560-572.

25. Taylor, Winnefred P. and Kenneth C. Hoedt, "Classroom Related Behavior Problems: Counsel Parents, Teachers or Children?", <u>Journal of Counseling Psychology</u>, XXI (1974), 3-8.

26. Wunderlich, Ray C., "The Hyperactivity Complex", <u>Journal of Optometric Vision Development,</u> VIII (March, 1977), 8-45.

27. Wunderlich, Ray C., "Paranoid Schizophrenia as a Manifestation of Metabolic Derangement: Successful Management by Metabolic Therapy", <u>Journal of the International Academy of Preventive Medicine</u>, III (September, 1976), 21-36.

Chapter 5

CASE STUDIES

Case Study #1:
    Female
    Age 30
    Attention Deficit Disorder, Hyperactive, Alcoholic

Mary was a hyperactive child. Her father and grandfather were alcoholics. She could not sit still or pay attention to her work in school. She looked out of the window instead of doing her work. In grade school she spent time in the hall and in the principal's office for disturbing the class. In Jr. High School she was more interested in socializing than in studies. In High School she skipped school and did not turn in her homework on any regular basis.

Mary drank alcohol and began experimenting with drugs and cigarettes. Since she was anxious most of the time, the alcohol and cigarettes made her feel calm and gave her a sense of well being. They also gave her a sense of belonging in a group of young people who were doing the same thing.

After Mary graduated from high school she moved to an apartment and took a job as a waitress and bartender. Her alcohol and drug use increased.

She attended junior college and earned a certificate as a legal assistant. She had several jobs which came to an end sooner or later because of alcohol abuse. A psychiatrist gave her various drugs which he thought would help her stop drinking. As a matter of fact, they kept her drinking and she was arrested for driving while intoxicated. She was taken to jail. Her depression caused her to drink more and use cocaine. After seizures she became suicidal due to drug and alcohol use.

Three beCALM'd and 2 grams of vitamin C had a positive effect in one hour's time. From then on she took vitamins, minerals and beCALM'd. She avoided caffeine and sugar and stopped drinking alcohol and using drugs.

Today, Mary works as a paralegal gathering information for lawyers so that they can try their cases.

She recently married and works out several times a week at a health club and has joined sailing club. Thanks to amino acids, healthy eating habits and nutritional supplements Mary has a normal life. She has been free of alcohol and drugs for 5 years.

Case Study #2:
> **Male**
>
> **Age 8**
>
> **Attention Deficit Disorder**
>
> **Hyperactive**

Jack was a child who could not get along with others at home or at school. He disrupted the life of his family at home and would not mind his parents. At school he did not follow instructions, or finish his work, and he was prone to emotional outbursts.

The following test results show that Jack had many deficiencies and abnormalities. These abnormalities were so severe that they greatly affected his behavior.

In the case of the ADHD child there are many deficiencies. The following describes test that were done on Jack, who suffered from attention deficit and hyperactivity:

Hair Analysis:

Low: Magnesium, Potassium, Iron, Manganese, Chromium, Selenium
High: Copper

Histamine:	9 Low (25 - 65 ng. ml.)	
Red Cell Vitamins:	B6 Low	
	Folic Acid Low	
	Vitamin A Low	
Ammonia:	46 High (11 - 35)	
Calcium:	8.8 Low (9.0 - 10.8)	
Fatty Acids		
Low: Myristic	0.32 (0.46 - 1.55)	High: Palmitic 1.95 (0.62 - 1.68)
Eicosapentaenoic	0.20 (0.26 - 1.56)	Stearic 2.19 (0.56 1.59)
Docosahexaenoic	0.30 (0.54 - 1.52)	
Linoleic	0.12 (0.66 - 2.18)	

Gamma Linolenic	0.08 (0.14 - 3.03)	
Arachidonic	0.35 (0.62 - 1.66)	
Myristoleic	0.01 (0.62 - 1.44)	
Palmitoleic	0.30 (0.46 - 1.74)	
Nervonic	0.18 (0.46 - 2.55)	
Palmitelaidic	0.14 (0.17 - 2.56)	

Cytotoxic Food Test

Reactive to goat milk, cow milk, cottage cheese, beef, pork, tuna fish, shrimp, turkey, rice, barley, cotton seed, soy bean, grapefruit, pineapple, lettuce, potato, pea, string bean, onion, mushroom, coffee, tea, malt, brewer's yeast, chive, clove, mustard, ginger, vanilla, beet sugar, cane sugar, scallop, oyster, banana, coconut, pear, red currant, plum, date, fig, blackberry, blueberry, raspberry, cranberry, carrot, sweet potato, turnip, kidney bean, navy bean, pinto bean, mint, olive, nutmeg, paprika, cinnamon, and almond.

24 Hour Urine for Amino Acids

Low: Threonine	60 mcm/24 hr.	(85 - 440)
Serine	148 mcm/24 hr.	(160 - 700)
Asparagine	25 mcm/24 hr.	(270 - 700)
Glutamic Acid	7 mcm/24 hr.	(55 - 270)
A-Aminoadipic Acid	24 mcm/24 hr.	(31 - 81)
Valine	13 mcm/24 hr.	(14 - 51)
Methionine	15 mcm/24 hr.	(20 - 95)
Cystathionine	trace	(20 - 95)
Isoleucine	7 mcm/24 hr.	(21 - 200)
Tyrosine	38 mcm/24 hr.	(40 - 270)

Jack came because he was hyperactive with violent behavior and attention deficit. He had been asked to leave two schools. He did not like to read and had impaired speech. He talked very fast and did not speak clearly. He ate hamburgers, cookies, chocolate milk, hot dogs, fried chicken and pizza. He drank sugared drinks such as Dr. Pepper, Coke, Pepsi and Big Red. He ate lots of sweets: skittles, ice cream, popsicles, snickers, and Hershey bars.

Jack began to eat nutritious food, leaving off junk foods and sweets. He took vitamins, minerals, alpha ketoglutaric acid, Evening Primrose Oil and a small amount of Ritalin. This treatment caused a dramatic change in Jack's behavior. He got along with his family and friends better. He could speak more clearly. He had more energy and better handwriting. He did not get into trouble at school, and he finished his work, making mostly A's and B's.

Cast Study #3:

Male

Age 10

Attention Deficit Disorder, Hyperactive

Tom began the year by being in the wrong place, doing the wrong things, cursing, hitting other children, sticking his fingers in other people's food, making loud noises, crushing his food and throwing it on the floor, breaking toys, stealing, lying not responding to requests, complaining, whining, and putting his fingers in his mouth. He hit another child right between the eyes with a rock. When he was corrected he made a face and shook his hands like an autistic child.

His mother and grandmother were alcoholic. His clothes were dirty and torn., his hair was not washed and he got lice. He was always hungry. Of course, he had no friends.

A physician tested Tom and found that he was excreting 7 times the normal amount of ammonia and he had a high score on the Yeast Questionnaire. He was allergic to bakers yeast, malt, milk, brewers yeast and cane sugar. He was given beCALM'd, acidophilus, capricin, vitamin C and a hypoallergenic multivitamin mineral. He stopped using sugar, fruit juice and milk.

The change was remarkable. He could do art work, read books, tell stories and play games without disrupting the activity. He actually sat quietly without squirming in the movie. His grades improved markedly. However, when he ate sugar or drank milk, his behavior deteriorated. For the first time, Tom learned what it felt like to make As and Bs.

Case Study #4
   Female
   Age 14
   Attention Deficit Disorder, Hyperactive

When Linda was a little girl she was hyperactive and impulsive. She had nightmares, wet her bed and heard voices. She had severe infections with fevers as high as 107. She had chronic bronchitis, pneumonia, ear and throat infections, and doctors gave her lots of antibiotics.

Linda could not sit still or pay attention in school. She had dyslexia and could barely read. Linda's behavior fluctuated between good and terrible. She was a female Dr. Jekyll and Mr. Hyde. In the fifth grade she had stomachaches, diarrhea and vomiting. In Junior High School she had mononucleosis twice and was in bed for weeks.

Linda took some tests: a urinalysis, an EEG, a hair analysis, a Cytotoxic Food Test, a 6 Hour Glucose Tolerance Test and a test for thyroid and pituitary hormones. She was found to have an abnormal EEG, abnormal blood sugar, food allergies, mineral imbalance and she was excreting cryptopyrrole (indicating a B_6 deficiency).

She was taken off of allergic foods, put on a diet void of sugar and milk, high in protein, and moderate in complex carbohydrates and fiber. She took nutritional supplements, including a multi-vitamin, mineral, extra B6, calcium, magnesium and zinc. She exercised several times a week.

One summer Linda read 20 books for recreation. Linda is much healthier. Her anger and mood changes have disappeared. The following table shows impressive changes in Linda's achievement.

	I.T.B.S. GRADE 5 Percentile	C.T.B.S. GRADE 8 Percentile	C.T.B.S. GRADE 9 Percentile
Reading Vocabulary	4	34	71
Reading Comprehension	28	82	89
Reading Total	28	65	82
Spelling	13	31	46
Math Problems	10	88	90
Language Usage	6	90	82
Reference	11	88	91

Case Study #5:

Male

Age 8

Hyperactive, Attention Deficit Disorder

Jim was taking 10 mg. of Ritalin three times a day. Taking Ritalin kept him from being hungry. He was thin and had not gained weight like the typical 8 year old. He could not go to sleep until 11:30 or 12:00 at night. He had emotional outbursts at times.

He was eating the following sweets: popsicle, pop-tart, peanut butter, ice cream, frozen yogurt, cake, cookies, regular sodas, Kool Aid, iced tea with sugar.

His mother cut the dose of Ritalin in half. He had been taking 10 mg. three times a day. He began to take beCALM'd, Therapeutic Vitamin (Bronson), vitamin C 250 mg., Evening Primrose Oil 500 mg. and Calcium, Magnesium, Boron and Zinc. In three days, Jim was off of Ritalin. He was eating normally. His mother said that he had barely been eating. Now he wanted to eat everything, and he was no longer finicky about what he ate.

In two more days, he was going to sleep by 9:30 and was able to get up in the morning and in a good mood. He was easy to get up. He had no emotional outbursts, and was more even tempered and easy to reason with.

In a month, he had grown in height and had gained two pounds. He did not cry anymore, bite his nails or have mood swings. He was doing better in school, according to his teacher.

Case Study #6

Male

Age 14

Alcohol and Drug Abuse, Schizophrenia, Hyperactivity, Learning Disability

Tommy was 14 years old. He drank beer, rum and whiskey and smoked marijuana. His behavior and school work deteriorated. He was angry and depressed. He made everyone in his family miserable. He had bad dreams and hallucinations. He was hospitalized for several months and given stelazine. After Tommy was released from the hospital he was antisocial and depressed. His father began to spend more time away from home, so that we would not have to be around Tommy. It was decided that Tommy would be sent to a psychiatric hospital for long term care. Before that happened, however, Tommy was brought to our office for testing. He was angry, depressed and negative. Tests showed that Tommy had high histamine and that he was allergic to grass, soy, yeast, chicken, banana, corn and oats. In talking with his mother I learned that Tommy's maternal grandmother was paranoid schizophrenic and that his mother was allergic.

Tommy scored 105 on the Harper Inventory for Hypoglycemic (a symptom survey) with complaints such as fatigue, fits of anger, depression, and suicidal thoughts. His score on the Yeast Questionnaire was 161 which far exceeded a normal score.

Tommy was asked not to use sugar, milk, milk products or fruit juice. He was given nystatin and appropriate vitamins and minerals.

When Tommy returned in three weeks he did not look or act like the same person. He was polite, subdued, and showed no signs of anger. He even laughed. His scores on the symptom survey and the yeast questionnaire had become normal.

	7/25/85	8/15/85
Harper Inventory	105	28
Yeast Questionnaire	161	38

Tommy continued to take supplements and to be careful about his diet. He remained sober and continued showing positive behavior. He began to show interest for the first time in a long time in activities such as drawing and painting and playing games. He was able to get up early in the morning and he did well in school.

Case Study #7

Male

age 25

Attention Deficit Hyperactive Disorder, Obsessive Compulsive

James was placed in some special education classes throughout his school years. He graduated from high school with a special degree.

As a child, James was hyperactive having temper fits when be did not get his way. When his parents divorced and sold their home James was so angered that he threw a brick through a stained glass window in their home. He was prone to outbursts of anger and once closed his mother in the closet and held her there. His father was an alcoholic and sometimes he and James would have physical fights. He had no friends.

James could not go to sleep at night until sometimes 2:00 AM, and then he would get up the next day around 12:00. He told lies and stole things that he wanted. He could not pay attention well enough to do what he was told to do. When he played tennis, he mumbled to himself and could not keep his eye on the ball or get the ball over the net with consistency. His father could always beat him in tennis. When asked to do something, he would reply that "he would do it in a little while". He got several jobs, but was fired from all of them.

Then James started to take Z-Plex, Calcium, Magnesium, Zinc, vitamin C and specially formulated vitamin mineral amino acid capsule called beCALM'd. He stopped eating sugar and using caffeine and fruit juice. He paid attention to eating salads, vegetables, grains, fruits and lean meats.

Three years later great changes have taken place in James's behavior. He is able to get up and go to work, sometimes as early as 7:00 AM. He has been employed in the same place for two years. His supervisors say that he is doing a very good job and they consider him a very hard worker. Recently he received an award for outstanding ability to be of service to customers. He is polite and well mannered.

James has had no temper outbursts. He used to eat huge quantities of food and even steal food from other people. He has, in fact, lost weight and does not eat nearly as much as he used to. The most amazing changes have taken place in his tennis game. He beats his father (and everybody else) at tennis. His ability to pay attention to hitting the ball and to place it away from his opponent is fascinating.

James is polite and cooperative, and he does not push to get his way like he used to. He has new friends.

The addition to his daily supplements of 480 mg. DHA from fish oil have made even more improvements in his functioning, handwriting and behavior.

Case Study #8:

> **Female**
>
> **Age 20**
>
> **Hyperactive, Alcoholic, Major Depression**

Jane's grandmother is a diabetic. Her father and uncle were alcoholic before they died. They allowed Jane to drink brandy, gin, vodka and tequila on special days since she was a child. By the time Jane was in her late teens, she was smoking two packages of cigarettes each day and drinking excessive amounts of alcohol. She also drank lots of Cokes.

Jane came with the following complaints: nervous stomach, hyperactive, not hungry, biting nails, throwing up food, fearful, anxious, lack of pleasure, fatigue, violent, sleep disturbance, lack of feelings, severe depression, inability to work and thoughts of suicide.

Jane was asked not to use alcohol, caffeine, sugar, or fruit juice. She was told to eat fresh vegetables, soups, salads, grains, fish, turkey, chicken, and other lean meat. She was asked to drink herb tea with Sweet 'N Low, bottled water and only one Diet Coke each day. She took the following supplements:

With breakfast:

1 1,000 mg. Vitamin C

1 Calcium, Magnesium, Zinc

1 Super B (Bronson)

10:00 A.M.

> 2 beCALM'd

3:00 P.M.

> 2 beCALM'd

9:00 P.M.

> 2 beCALM'd
>
> 1 1,00 mg. Vitamin C
>
> 1 500 mg. GABA

In seven weeks Jane returned. The changes in her were remarkable. She was calm and could sit still. She smiled, laughed and even made jokes. She was no longer violent or depressed, and she was able to sleep at night. Her feelings for self, others and God had returned. She no longer felt badly about herself and wanted to be alone. She felt much better and had more energy. She had gone back to work.

In subsequent visits, Jane continued to improve. She quit biting her nails. She no longer drank alcohol and had cut her cigarette smoking in half.

Chapter 6

ELIMINATE SUGAR

Perhaps the best thing you can do for your health is to eliminate sugar from your diet. If you do this you will have more energy, you will have fewer infections and you will be less likely to be depressed.

The reason I know that this is so is that I have experienced it myself. I have observed others who gave up sugar, as well. The result of this action has always been positive. In some cases, the change was remarkable.

I used to be tired, especially in the afternoons. I had migraine headaches in college. I also had many bladder infections and strep throats. As a young adult, I had bronchitis and pneumonia several times. Doctors gave me antibiotics again and again. I got yeast infections many times and suffered from depression.

I attended nutrition classes at SMU. The instructor said that if I would give up sugar, that in six weeks it would not taste good. He was right. About six weeks from the time I stopped eating sugar, I tasted a piece of wedding cake with frosting. It really did not taste good. It was sickeningly sweet.

Due to eliminating sugar and alcohol and taking nutritional supplements, I am no longer plagued by migraine headaches, bladder infections and strep throat infections. I have not had repeated bouts of bronchitis and pneumonia. I don't take antibiotics or have yeast infections. This is truly a blessing.

The only way to keep from eating sugar is not to buy it or have it in your house. You have to read labels on prepared foods. When you buy fresh fruits, vegetables and grains you are not exposed to great quantities of sugar, so try to do most of your shopping in the fresh produce department of the grocery store.

HARMFUL EFFECTS OF SUGAR

The American Journal of Clinical Nutrition published in 1973 the results of a study. A group of individuals was given sucrose and fructose. There was, in all test subjects, a decrease in the capacity of the neutrophils (white blood cells) to kill bacteria. The effect lasted for five hours.

If you eat sugar morning, afternoon and evening, you can wipe out your body's defense system. Then, when you are exposed to harmful bacteria your body will not be able to defend itself. It is no surprise that many children get sick the day after Halloween, Thanksgiving, and Christmas following the ingestion of large quantities of sugared foods.

Sugar can act like a drug. As you decrease the amount you consume, you may experience withdrawal symptoms including irritability, headaches, nausea and anxiety. These symptoms occur because your blood sugar drops and the brain is not well fed. Drink lots of liquids such as herb teas and filtered water. Eat several small meals each day containing protein and complex carbohydrates.

Make a seed mix composed of one part raw pumpkin seeds, one part raw sunflower seeds and two parts roasted and salted soy nuts. (These are distributed by American Natural Snacks, St. Augustine, FL. 32085) put in snack size ziplock bags and store in the refrigerator. Snack on this seed mix during the day. Also, make a shake containing 10 oz. soy milk, 1 tsp. almond butter, ½ banana, 1 scoop whey protein powder and Stevia Plus or one hard boiled Omega-3 fortified egg, sugar free apple sauce and 3 almonds. This will help calm your sugar cravings.

Once you are free from sugar, you will feel more calm and relaxed. You will think more clearly and sleep better. Also, you will have more energy.

When you are reading labels avoid products that contain sucrose, corn syrup, dextrose, maltose, and glucose. These are all sugars.

Chapter 7

WHAT TO EAT

The important thing to remember about food is to pick high nutrient food such as fresh or steamed vegetables, fresh fruits, whole grains, nuts, lean meats, and good fats such as those found in olive oil and avocado. Buy organically grown food, if possible and sun ripened (not picked green) fruits and vegetables so that you get the health promoting benefits of the phytochemicals they contain. Phytochemicals are the general name for plant synthesized molecules, which help the body to heal itself.

Do not use sugar, caffeine, or fruit juice. If you have a juicer, however, do drink fresh vegetable juices, as they are full of nutrients. Eat some protein with complex carbohydrates and unsaturated fat at each meal, and plan healthy snacks between meals. Be sure to drink eight glasses of water a day, as water is hydrating and good for the immune system. Soda pop and alcohol are dehydrating. Soda pop contains phosphoric acid, which turns your body fluids acid and makes you tired.

Remember that what you eat and drink feeds your cells and keeps you in a state of good health. If you select foods that have been picked green or have been sprayed with pesticides, food that is full of sugar or drinks that contain chemicals you are robbing your body of nutrients.

Food suggestions follow:

Use butter – or Smart Balance

Use olive oil on salads and Puritan Oil (canola oil) to cook with.

Do not use sugar or fruit juice.

To sweeten food and drinks use:

{ Stevia Plus   { fresh or dried fruit

{ Xylitol   { Xylo Sweet

BREAD	CEREALS	OTHER
rye	grape nuts	Omega-3 enriched eggs, guacamole, apple
whole grain bread	shredded wheat squares	low fat cottage cheese, fruit, Smart Balance Mayonnaise
sprouted grain bread	hot oatmeal (slow cooked)	melons, deli turkey, 4 Macademia nuts
English muffin	hot barley cereal	grapefruit, protein shake, 6 almonds
pumpernickel rye	cous cous	string cheese, crackers, 6 olives
SALADS		
melons	cabbage slaw	pear, grated cheese, Smart Balance Mayonnaise, cottage cheese
sliced tomatoes	apple, pecan, celery	grilled chicken salad
lettuce, tomato, avocado, cucumber with freshly squeezed lemon juice		
VEGETABLES (Fresh, Steamed, Baked or Raw)		
lentils	cauliflower	black eyed peas
lima beans	broccoli	green beans
turnip greens	baked acorn squash	brussels sprouts
egg plant	yellow squash	asparagus
celery	zucchini squash	spinach
kidney beans	okra	peas
onions	cabbage	beans (black, pinto, navy)
MEATS		
swiss steak	broiled fish (salmon)	pork chop
broiled lamb chops	rock cornish hen	chicken
meat loaf	baked turkey	ham
broiled steak	ribs	brisket
DRINKS		
filtered water	Perrier & fresh lime	Clamato
club soda & lemon	sugar free Winterbrook Seltzer	
carrot & celery juice, (fresh)	Beefamato	
BIGELOW HERB TEAS	cranberry apple	country peach
	red raspberry	orange & spice
CELESTIAL SEASONS Teas	lemon zinger	strawberry kiwi
	wild cherry blackberry	peppermint
TREATS		
plums	toasted spelt waffle	black olives
cherries	Cinnamon raisin Ezekiel toast	raw veggies
plain yogurt & berries	tortilla chips & salsa	peanuts
pecans, cashews	toasted Ezekiel bread	grapes
cantaloupe	English muffin	watermelon
almonds	honey dew melon	peaches
peanut butter & crackers	strawberries	apples

EXAMPLES

BREAKFAST:

      2 Omega-3 fortified eggs scrambled

      2 Tablespoons guacamole

      2 Tablespoons salsa

      1 cup unsweetened applesauce with cinnamon

LUNCH:

      4 ounces turkey breast

      with 2 Tablespoons guacamole on rye bread (sandwich)

DINNER:

      4 ounces skinless chicken breast broiled

      1 1/4 cups broccoli

      1 cup kidney beans

      1 cup fresh strawberries

      4 teaspoons slivered almonds

SNACKS:

      1 Macadamia nut1/2 cup tomato soup   (mid-morning)

      1 ounce lean ham

      1 ounce turkey breast   (afternoon)

      1/2 apple

      3 black olives

      2 ounces low-fat cottage cheese   (before bed)

      1/2 cup blueberries

      3 almonds

  **for complete information see <u>Mastering the Zone</u> and <u>Zone Perfect Meals In Minutes</u> by Barry Sears, Ph.D.

Chapter 8

NUTRITIONAL SUPPLEMENTS

I have been taking a variety of nutritional supplements for years. Taking nutritional supplements and leaving off sugars and alcohol have improved the quality of my life in many ways. I rarely get sick or go to the doctor. I have not taken antibiotics in years. I have plenty of energy and generally feel very well. I can read and process information much faster than I could when I was young because my brain works better.

The body requires all the vitamins, minerals, amino acids and fatty acids to work properly. A deficiency of one nutrient can cause problems. Several deficiencies can set off a chain of very unfortunate events resulting in many unwanted symptoms.

The medical literature clearly indicates that hyperactive children have a deficiency of serotonin, that they have abnormal carbohydrate metabolism causing low levels of blood sugar and ineffective feeding of the brain. Sometimes they have abnormal levels of hormones, a need for more vitamins, deficiency of Omega-3 fatty acids, as well as zinc, chromium and magnesium and reactions to foods and chemicals. Kenneth Blum, Ph. D. at the University of Texas Health Science Center, with Noble and Sheridan discovered a 6.6-Kb fragment of the gene for the Dopamine D2 Receptor and found that it was highly associated with alcoholism (the A_1 allele). The children of alcoholics (who are often hyperactive) were tested by Olivier Civelli and his group. The A_1 allele of the dopamine D2 receptor gene was found in 39 children. A person who has the A_1 allele has a shortage of dopamine receptors and will be likely to seek alcohol in times of stress to give him relief. This suggests some alcoholism is genetic [1].

Dr. Blum designed the vitamin, mineral, amino acid formulation called "SAAVE", which has been modified to relate also to stress and ADHD associated deficiencies and is now called "beCALM'd"™. The use of beCALM'd is an amino acid loading technique which improves brain nutrition and function. It has been used successfully with children of alcoholics, those with ADD, hyperactivity, ADHD and addicts to improve feeling states, brain function, and behavior. In alcoholics, it helps diminish cravings for alcohol [2].

SUGGESTIONS CONCERNING NUTRITIONAL SUPPLEMENTATION

There are many companies that make nutritional supplements. When selecting supplements, make sure that they are "hypoallergenic - yeast free". They should be free of cane sugar. Some children can tolerate fructose and others cannot. Nobody can say what is the best combination for you or your child to take.

I am going to merely suggest some supplements that you or your child might try. A person can react badly to any substance. Therefore, it is a good idea to try one supplement at a time. Take one supplement. If it does not make you or your child feel badly, add another, and then another, etc. (take multivitamins with food and "beCALM'd" on an empty stomach). Children who have white spots on their fingernails, a sign of zinc deficiency, may need 15 to 30 mgs. of zinc daily for several months.

The following lists are of supplements that others have found to be beneficial:

SUGGESTED SUPPLEMENTS
Ages 3-5

With Breakfast:
- 1 Multi Vitamin Mineral Supplement
- ½ 250 mg. (chewable) Vitamin C
- Mix ½ tsp. pharmaceutical grade fish oil in 4 oz. V-8 and drink or mix fish oil in peanut butter or almond butter.

9:30 A.M.
- ½ - 1 Capsule beCALM'd

3:30 P.M.
- ½ - 1 Capsule beCALM'd
- ½ 250 mg (chewable) Vitamin C

9:30 P.M.
- ½-1 Capsule beCALM'd (if needed)

Multi-Vitamin Mineral

Phyto Bears (2-4) per day, (chewable) vitamin, mineral

Mannatech (800) 281-4469

Associate Number R64053

Children's Chewable Vitamins & Minerals (1) per day

Solaray (800) 669-8877

Nutritional Systems, P. O. Box 600, Santa Cruz, CA 95061

Vitamin C - 250 mg. (chewable, non acidic) #44

Bronson Pharmaceutical (800) 235-3200

beCALM'd

Neurogenesis (800) 232-7563 Distributor #12731

Pharmaceutical Grade Fish Oil

Dr. Sears Omega Rx Liquid, Nature's Pharmaceuticals,

Toll free (877) 879-3801.

SUGGESTED SUPPLEMENTS
Age 6-8

30 minutes before breakfast:
- 1 beCALM'd
- 1 250 mg. Vitamin C

With breakfast:
- 1 multi-vitamin mineral supplement (hypoallergenic) or (2-6 Phyto Bears)
- 1 Sublingual B-12, The TriVita Way, Distributor #11258978 (1 888 432-4829)
- 1/2 tsp. Pharmaceutical Grade Fish Oil in 4 oz. V-8 or mix fish oil in peanut butter or almond butter.

11:30 or 30 minutes before lunch:
- 1 beCALM'd

9:00 P.M.
- 1 - 2 beCALM'd
- 1 250 mg. Vitamin C
- 1 Calcium, Magnesium, Zinc

Multi Vitamin Mineral

Phyto Bears (2 - 6 per day) chewable vitamin mineral
        Mannatech (800) 281-4469
        Associate number R64053

Children's Chewable Vitamins & Minerals (2) per day
        Solaray (800) 669-8877

Vitamin C
250 mg (chewable, non acid) (product #44)
    Bronson Pharmaceutical; 800-235-3200

beCALM'd
    Neurogenesis (800) 232-7563 Distributor #12731

Calcium, Magnesium, Zinc (250, 150, 13)
    Natures Life - Health Food Store

Pharmaceutical Grade Fish Oil
    Dr. Sears Omega Rx Liquid, Nature's Pharmaceuticals,
    Toll free (877) 879-3801

Purified Fish Oil
    Nordic Naturals - Health Food Store

SUGGESTED SUPPLEMENTS
Age 9-11

30 minutes before breakfast:

- 2 beCALM'd

With breakfast:

- 1 multi-vitamin mineral supplement (hypoallergenic) or (2-6 Phyto Bears)
- 1 500 mg. Vitamin C
- 1 Sublingual B-12, The TriVita Way, Distributor #11258978 (1 888 432-4829)
- 1/2 tsp. Pharmaceutical Grade Fish Oil (240 mg. DHA) in 4 oz. V-8 or mix fish oil in peanut butter or almond butter.

30 minutes before lunch:

- 2 beCALM'd

9:30 P.M.

- 1-2 beCALM'd
- 1 500 mg. Vitamin C
- 1 Calcium, Magnesium, Zinc

Multi Vitamin Mineral
Daily One Caps; Twin Lab - Health Food Store
Therapeutic Formula - Formula #2
     Bronson Pharmaceutical; 800-235-3200

Vitamin C
Ester-C with Bioflavanoid Complex 500 mg.
     Natrol - Health Food Store

Zinc

      Zinc 15 mg. (Product #16)

      Bronson Pharmaceutical; 800-235-3200

Pharmaceutical Grade Fish Oil

      Dr. Sears Omega Rx Liquid, Nature's Pharmaceuticals,

      Toll free (877) 879-3801

Purified Fish Oil

      1 capsule Swanson EFA's Super EPA, item #P5SWE026

      Swanson Health Products, 800 437-4148

beCALM'd

      Neurogenesis (800) 232-7563 Distributor #12731

Calcium Magnesium Zinc

      Calcium Magnesium Boron Zinc (product #210)

      Bronson Pharmaceutical; 800 235-3200

SUGGESTED SUPPLEMENTS
Age 12 and over

With breakfast:
- 1 multi-vitamin mineral supplement (yeast-free, hypoallergenic)
- 1 Calcium Magnesium Zinc
- 1 1,000 mg. Vitamin C
- 1 Sublingual B-12, The Tri Vita Way, Distributor #11258978 (1 888 432-4829)
- 1 fish oil capsule

9:30 A.M. or 7:30 A.M.
- 2 beCALM'd

3:30 P.M.
- 1-2 beCALM'd

9:30 P.M.
- 2 beCALM'd
- 1 1,000 mg. Vitamin C
- 1 Calcium Magnesium Zinc (if needed)

Multi Vitamin Mineral

Daily One Caps; Twin Lab - Health Food Store

Therapeutic Formula (product #2); Bronson Pharmaceutical; 800-235-3200

Calcium Magnesium Zinc

Calcium (250 mg.) Magnesium (150 mg.) Zinc (13 mg.) (product #210)
    Bronson Pharmaceutical; 800-235-3200

Calcium (250 mg.) Magnesium (150 mg.) Zinc (13 mg.); Natures Life - Health Food Store

Vitamin C

Vitamin C 1,000 mg. (product #47); Bronson Pharmaceutical; 800-235-3200

Allergy C Caps (Buffered C); Twin Lab - Health Food Store

beCALM'd

Neurogenesis (800) 232-7563 Distributor #12731

Purified Fish Oil

1 capsule Swanson EFA's Super EPA, item #P5SWE026

Swanson Health Products, 800 437-4148

CHAPTER BIBLIOGRAPHY

1. Blum, Kenneth, <u>Alcohol and the Addictive Brain</u>, The Free Press, New York, 1991.

2. Burgess, J.R.; L. Stevens; W. Zhang; and L. Peck. "Long-Chain polyunsaturated fatty acids in children with attention deficit hyperactivity disorder". <u>American Journal of Clinical Nutrition</u> 71(2000): 3275-3305.

3. Neher, Terry, "Neuronutrient Therapy: A study in Stabilizing The Stress of Recovery", <u>Professional Counselor</u>, August 1993, 27, 28, 53.

4. Regelson, William, <u>The Super Hormone Promise,</u> Pocket Books, New York, 1996.

5. Sears, Barry, <u>The Omega Rx Zone</u>, Regan Books, New York, 2002.

6. Stevens, Laura, et al, "Essential Fatty Acid Metabolism in Boys with Attention-Deficit Hyperactivity Disorder", <u>American Journal of Clinical Nutrition</u>, 62, (1995), 761-768.

7. Stoll, Andrew, <u>The Omega-3 Connection</u>, Simon and Schuster New York, 2001.

8. Stordy, Jacqueline, <u>The LCP Solution</u>, Ballantine Books, New York, 2000.

TO ORDER SUPPLEMENTS

To order supplements comparable to those listed in this book (except for beCALM'd and sublingual B-12) call:

Swanson Health Products for a catalog at (800) 437-4148.

Chapter 9

OTHER THINGS TO DO

Our food, water, air and soil are being bombarded by chemicals, molds, fungi, bacteria and pollens. Even our homes have chemicals, dust and gasses that invade our living space. When too many of these substances accumulate in our environment, they evoke unwanted responses such as fatigue, depression, sneezing, watery eyes, congestion and brain fog. Cleaning up the environment will reduce the number and severity of symptoms.

DRINK CLEAN WATER

To protect yourself and your family you can reduce the load of unhealthy substances to which you are exposed. You can also enhance your immune system by drinking filtered water. Water is hydrating and is helpful to the immune system. It also helps to alkalinize body fluids, causing a person to be more energetic. Alcoholic beverages, caffeinated drinks and soda pop are dehydrating and cause a loss of nutrients. They also are acid forming, taking away one's energy.

There are several kinds of water filters. Most people say that reverse osmosis provides the most effective water filtration of any system available today. In order to have pure, good tasting water that comes out of the kitchen faucet you can purchase a counter top filtration unit. There are also filters which can be attached to your shower head. These are carbon filters. The filters removed chlorine, minerals and bacteria, making the water more healthful. Units with carbon filters are the least expensive, but it is necessary to change the filters more often.

EAT NUTRITIOUS FOODS

Purchase vegetables and fruits that are free of pesticides. Also, select fresh foods that are vine ripened so that they contain healing phytochemicals. Wash fruits and vegetables thoroughly and eat them raw or steamed topped with spices such as oregano, onion and garlic. Pouring a little olive oil on the vegetables before they are steamed adds to the taste.

PREVENT EXPOSURE TO MERCURY

It is best to have your dentist fill teeth with composite (white) instead of amalgam (silver). It has been demonstrated to me that removing amalgam fillings can restore a sense of health, good balance, and well being. Mercury is toxic. Hal Huggins, a dentist from Colorado Springs, Colorado has written about the fact that mercury has been shown to pass into the blood from the amalgam filling. He has restored health to people with various illnesses by removing their amalgam fillings and replacing them with composite.

Children are especially sensitive to the mercury contained in amalgam fillings. Some children have complained of severe headache until the fillings were removed and replaced with composite.

AVOID CONTAMINANTS

If you are allergic you may obtain a little relief by avoiding gas heat, cigarette smoke, solvents and cleaning products containing ammonia. Many people react to perfumes, feather pillows, plastics, animal fur and outgassing synthetic carpets. These things have the ability to make some people sick.

USE BRIGHT LIGHT THERAPY

Dr. Norman Rosenthal studied seven children (less than 18 years of age) who experienced sadness, anxiety, or irritability during the winter months accompanied by at least three of the following symptoms: fatigue, sleep changes, increased or decreased appetite, carbohydrate craving or headaches. All subjects experienced school difficulties or social withdrawal. A trial of bright environmental light reversed many of the symptoms and improved mood and social functioning. Typically 30 minutes a day in front of a light providing 10,000 lux at 14 inches is effective.

You can purchase Sun Ray, a bright light box with a stand which can be placed on a desk. It is a UV-free light, providing 10,000 lux at 14 inches. The cost is $399.00 plus shipping.

To order, call or write:

The Sun Box Company
19217 Orbit Drive
Gaithersburg, MD 20879
(800) 548-3968

GET HYDRATED

Drink one 8 oz. glass of filtered water 30 minutes before each meal. Drink little with the meal. Starting 2 hours after the meal drink 8 oz. water each hour and drink during the night. You have sufficient water when the urine is free of yellow color. You can drink some herb teas with Stevia, however, do not drink soda pop, coffee, tea or alcohol, as they are dehydrating. According to Dr. Batmanghelidj, your body is powered by water. Being hydrated will enhance the immune system, give you energy and increase the serotonin level in the brain. This information comes from his book, <u>Your Body's Many Cries for Water</u>.

IF YOU WANT TO OMIT PILLS AT BREAKFAST

Make a shake in the blender... Put one scoop of chocolate or vanilla Atkins shake mix in the blender with 12 ounces of cold filtered water, 2 tsp. Unflavored Nutri-Quick, Twenty First Century Products, (940) 243-2178, 1 Tbls. High Lignan Flax Oil per hundred pounds of body weight. Add Stevia or Sweet 'N Low, if desired, and blend on high speed. Take required fish oil before bed.

LEARN ABOUT SEROTONIN

Symptoms of Low Serotonin
- Sleep disturbance
- Irritability
- Depressed
- Hard to get up in the morning

♦ Hyperactive

♦ Attention Deficit

♦ Lying

♦ Stealing (Kleptomania)

♦ Headaches

♦ Want to be Left Alone

♦ Sudden Tears

♦ Lack of Feelings

♦ Unusually Susceptible to pain

♦ Problems Concentrating

♦ Cravings for sugar or alcohol

♦ Temper outbursts

♦ Shouting

♦ Hurting others

♦ Violent behavior

♦ Suicide attempts

To Increase Serotonin:

a)   Take Omega-3 Fatty Acids found in fish oil

b)   Take 40 mg. B-6 daily

c)   Take 500 mg. L-Tryptophan 2 times a day, or

d)   Take 50 mg. 5-HTP 2 times a day

e)   Take 20-30 mg. Zinc daily

f)   Take 2 capsules beCALM'd 2 or 3 times a day

g)   Do not use sugar, fruit juice or alcohol

h)   Follow diet suggestions in <u>Mastering the Zone</u> by Barry Sears

i)   Exercise by walking 30 minutes 4 times a week

j)   Get hydrated … Drink 8 ounces of water each hour (except when eating) … drink enough so that your urine has no yellow color … wait 2 hours after a meal to drink … drink 30 minutes before each meal and during the night.

CHAPTER BIBLIOGRAPHY

1. Atkins, Robert C., <u>Dr Atkins' New Diet Revolution</u>, Avon Books, New York, New York, 1992.

2. Batmanghelidj, F., "Pain: A Need for Paradigm Change", <u>Anticancer Research</u>, (1987) 972-990.

3. Batmanghelidj, F., <u>Your Body's Many Cries For Water</u>, Global Health Solutions, Falls Church, Virginia.

4. Bhagavan, Hemige N., Mary Coleman, and David Baird Coursin, "The Effect of Pyridoxine Hydrochloride on Blood Serotonin and Pyridoxal Phosphate Contents in Hyperactive Children", <u>Pediatrics</u>, LV (March, 1975), 437-446.

5. Hibbein, Joseph R., "Fish consumption and major depression", <u>The Lancet</u>, 351 (1998): 1213.

6. Sears, Barry, <u>Mastering the Zone</u>, Regan Books, New York, New York, 1997.

7. Toren, et al., "Zinc Deficiency in Attention Deficit Hyperactivity Disorder", <u>Biological Psychiatry</u> 40 (1996): 1308-1310.

Chapter 10

QUESTIONNAIRES

If you feel that you or your child are suffering from hyperactivity check the symptoms you have on the Hyperactivity Symptom List. If the score is more than 10, there may be a problem.

If you think your child is hyperactive fill out the Conners Parent Questionnaire. If you check mostly 2's and 3's your child may have a problem. Ask your child's teacher to fill out the questionnaire and you will have a better idea of his daily behavior.

On the "Feelings Assessment" circle the letter and number which is adjacent to any feeling that you experience on a regular basis. The letters stand for the following "o" = opiates, "g" = GABA, "d" = dopamine, "n" = norepinephrine, "s" = serotonin. These names refer to neurotransmitters or chemicals in the brain that make us feel "alive" and "good". If you circle more than two o's you are possibly low in opiates. If you circle more than two g's you are possibly low in GABA, etc. I have found in working with hyperactive youngsters and adults as well as alcoholics and addicts that it is not unusual for them to check every feeling on both pages. This means that their deficiencies and abnormalities keep their brains from working in a normal way and prevent them from having normal feelings. However, it is not uncommon to see the negative feelings disappear when they eliminate sugar and milk, eat nutritious foods, and take vitamins, minerals and "beCALM'd".

If you or your child circled more than nine of the feelings on the assessment the specially formulated vitamin, mineral, amino acid supplement called, "beCALM'd" should be helpful. It was designed to give the body the raw material it needs to manufacture neurotransmitters (chemicals in the brain) that make the brain function optimally. I have used these supplements for many years and have seen miraculous changes in those who take them, as well as in myself.

beCALM'd is made of natural substances and has no side effects if taken in appropriate doses. It helps one sleep, be calm, pay attention and be focused on work. It also helps reduce the effects of stress, keeps one from losing his temper and reduces cravings for alcohol and drugs. The effect of beCALM'd can be noticed often with the first dose. This supplement should be taken with vitamin C between meals for the best results.

Put a check in the blank opposite each symptom that you or your child has on the test labeled "Symptoms of Hypoglycemia". If the score is over 25 you most likely have a problem with fluctuating blood sugar. In order to stabilize the flow of glucose to the brain it is important to omit sweets, caffeine, alcohol and drugs. Eat three meals a day containing some protein and vegetables at least twice a day. Eat nutritious snacks between meals and drink plenty of filtered water. Take suggested nutritional supplements and then check the symptom sheet three weeks later. You should see the score drop and you should feel much better.

If you or your child has had infections, which have regularly been treated with antibiotics, you may have a problem. The problem could be that you have an overgrowth of Candida Albicans (yeast germ).

Antibiotics kill the friendly bacteria in the intestinal tract but the yeasts multiply, put out toxins and make you sick. They weaken your immune system causing fatigue and depression. Nutritional deficiencies and exposure to allergens also weaken the immune system.

Parents of children, who are hyperactive or have attention deficit disorder, answer the questions on the Yeast Questionnaire for Children. Dr. Crook says that if the score is 60 or more, yeasts probably play a role in your child's problems. If the score is 140 or more, yeasts almost certainly play a role in your child's health or problem behavior.

Adults answer the questions in the Yeast Questionnaire. Put the appropriate point score opposite each question. Add the totals for sections A, B and C.

Dr. Crook says that yeast-connected health problems are probably present in females with scores over 120 and in males with scores over 90.

If your score is in that range, stop using sugar, alcohol and soda pop. Take nutritional supplements plus Acidophilus and Yeast-Fighters (Twin Lab). Read The Yeast Connection Handbook by William Crook, M.D. and The Yeast Syndrome by John Parks Trowbridge, M.D.

In the 23 years that I have been using diets and nutritional supplements to help people with their problems, I have witnessed remarkable recoveries. If you or your child or loved one is experiencing difficulty, do not lose hope. Miracles are quite possible.

Hyperactivity Symptom List

1.)   Restless
2.)   Overactive
3.)   Short attention span
4.)   Low tolerance for frustration
5.)   Fights with others
6.)   Temper outbursts
7.)   Mood changes
8.)   Sleep disturbance
9.)   Unable to sleep for a full eight hours
10.)   Enuresis (bed wetting)
11.)   Fever
12.)   Aching
13.)   Sore throats
14.)   Stomachaches
15.)   Lying
16.)   Stealing
17)   Depression
18)   Often hungry
19)   Visual disturbance
20)   Headaches
21)   Fatigue
22)   Nausea
23)   Motion sickness
24)   Dizziness
25)   Ringing in the ears
26)   Enjoys sugared foods
27)   Reverses letters when reading or writing
28)   Cold hands and feet

29) Poor coordination

30) Allergies

31) Has trouble with school work

32) Abnormal EEG

33) Parents and/or grandparents have a history of alcoholism, hypoglycemia, diabetes, dyslexia, depression, schizophrenia or stroke.

CONNERS PARENT QUESTIONNAIRE

Listed below are items concerning children's behavior. Read each item carefully and decide how much you think your child has been bothered by this problem during this observation period.

			Not at all	Just a little	Pretty much	Very much
Problems of	1.	Picky and finicky	0	1	2	3
Eating	2.	Will not eat enough	0	1	2	3
	3.	Often hungry	0	1	2	3
Problems of	4.	Restless	0	1	2	3
Sleep	5.	Nightmares	0	1	2	3
	6.	Awakens at night	0	1	2	3
	7.	Cannot fall asleep	0	1	2	3
Fear and	8.	Afraid of new situations	0	1	2	3
Worries	9.	Afraid of people	0	1	2	3
	10.	Afraid of being alone	0	1	2	3
	11.	Worries about illness & death	0	1	2	3
Muscular	12.	Gets still and rigid	0	1	2	3
Tension	13.	Twitches, jerks, etc.	0	1	2	3
	14.	Shakes	0	1	2	3
Speech	15.	Stuttering	0	1	2	3
Problems	16.	Hard to understand	0	1	2	3
Wetting	17.	Bed wetting	0	1	2	3
	18.	Runs to bathroom	0	1	2	3
Bowel Problems	19.	Soiling self	0	1	2	3
	20.	Holds back bowel movements	0	1	2	3
Complaining of	21.	Headaches	0	1	2	3
Following Symptoms	22.	Stomachaches	0	1	2	3
Even though Doctor	23.	Vomiting	0	1	2	3
Finds nothing wrong	24.	Aches and Pains	0	1	2	3
	25.	Loose bowels	0	1	2	3
Problems of	26.	Sucks thumb	0	1	2	3
Sucking, chewing	27.	Bites or picks nails	0	1	2	3
Or picking	28.	Chews on clothes, blankets, etc.	0	1	2	3
	29	Picks at hair, clothing, etc.	0	1	2	3

			Not at all	Just a little	Pretty much	Very much
Inadequate	30.	Does not act his age	0	1	2	3
Maturation:	31.	Cries	0	1	2	3
	32.	Wants help doing things	0	1	2	3
	33.	Clings to parents or others	0	1	2	3
	34.	Baby talk	0	1	2	3
Trouble with Feelings	35.	Keeps anger to himself	0	1	2	3
	36.	Lets himself get pushed around by other children	0	1	2	3
	37.	Unhappy	0	1	2	3
	38.	Carries chip on his shoulder	0	1	2	3
Over-Asserts	39.	Bullying	0	1	2	3
Himself:	40.	Bragging and Boasting	0	1	2	3
	41.	Sassy to grown-ups	0	1	2	3
Problems	42.	Shy	0	1	2	3
Making	43.	Afraid they do not like him	0	1	2	3
Friends:	44.	Feelings easily hurt	0	1	2	3
	45	Has no friends	0	1	2	3
Problems with	46.	Feels cheated	0	1	2	3
Brothers and	47.	Mean	0	1	2	3
Sisters	48.	Fights	0	1	2	3
Problems	49.	Disturbs other children	0	1	2	3
Keeping	50.	Wants to run things	0	1	2	3
Friends	51.	Picks on other children	0	1	2	3
Restless	52.	Restless (over-active)	0	1	2	3
	53.	Excitable, impulsive	0	1	2	3
	54.	Fails to finish things (short attention span)	0	1	2	3
Temper	55.	Temper outbursts, explosive and unpredictable behavior	0	1	2	3
	56.	Throws himself around	0	1	2	3
	57.	Throws and breaks things	0	1	2	3
	58.	Pouts and sulks	0	1	2	3

			Not at all	Just a little	Pretty much	Very much
Sex	59.	Plays with own sex organs	0	1	2	3
	60.	Involved in sex play with others	0	1	2	3
	61.	Modest about his or her own body	0	1	2	3
Problems in School	62.	Learning is a problem	0	1	2	3
	63.	Does not like to go to school	0	1	2	3
	64.	Is afraid to go to school	0	1	2	3
	65.	Daydreams	0	1	2	3
	66.	Truancy	0	1	2	3
	67.	Will not obey school rules	0	1	2	3
Lying	68.	Denies having done wrong	0	1	2	3
	69.	Blames others for his mistakes	0	1	2	3
	70.	Tells stories which do not happen	0	1	2	3
Stealing	71.	From parents	0	1	2	3
	72.	At school	0	1	2	3
	73.	From stores and other places	0	1	2	3
Fire Setting	74	Set fires	0	1	2	3
Trouble with Police	75	Gets into trouble with police	0	1	2	3
Excessive or Compulsive	76.	Everything must be just so	0	1	2	3
	77.	Things must be done the same way every time	0	1	2	3
	78.	Sets goals to high	0	1	2	3

			Not at all	Just a little	Pretty much	Very much
Additional	79.	Inattentive, easily distracted	0	1	2	3
Problems	80.	Fidgeting	0	1	2	3
	81.	Cannot be left alone	0	1	2	3
	82.	Climbing, gets into things	0	1	2	3
	83.	A very early riser	0	1	2	3
	84.	Will run around between mouthfuls at meals	0	1	2	3
	85.	Demands must be met immediately - easily frustrated	0	1	2	3
	86.	Cannot stand too much excitement	0	1	2	3
	87.	Laces & zippers are open	0	1	2	3
	88.	Cries	0	1	2	3
	89.	Unable to stop a repetitive activity	0	1	2	3
	90.	Acts as if driven by a motor	0	1	2	3
	91.	Mood changes very quickly	0	1	2	3
	92.	Poorly aware of surroundings or time	0	1	2	3
	93.	Clumsy				
	94.	How serious a problem do you think your child has at this time?	None	Minor	Moderate	Severe

SYMPTOMS OF HYPOGLYCEMIA

1. At time my mind goes blank

2. I become easily confused

3. I am forgetful

4. Occasionally I have difficulty with concentration

5. I am an underachiever now in school or in work

6. I lose my temper easily

7. I have difficulty in controlling my emotions

8. I have excessive sexual desires

9. (Male) I am impotent. (Female) I am frigid.

10. I neglect cleanliness and appearance.

11. I have difficulty in keeping my jobs.

12. I am very impatient.

13. I cannot get along with others easily.

14. Certain things irritate me very much.

15. I am depressed, blue

16. I lost interest in my work.

17. I am tired of living.

18. I am very nervous.

19. My life has become aimless.

20. I am anxious and afraid but I do not know why.

21. I have a feeling of impending danger.

22. I feel very tense.

23. I have groundless fears (phobias).

24. I have crying spells.

25. I feel very restless.

26. I have suicidal tendencies.

27. I easily become violent.

28. I have a desire to cause damage to others.

29. I want revenge on society.

30. My vision occasionally becomes blurred or double.

31. Sunlight hurts my eyes.

32. I feel dizzy, stagger, or weave especially in the a.m. or before meals.

33. I feel dizzy or blackout especially when I stand up suddenly.

34. I am very exhausted, especially in the morning.

35. I generally feel very tired and weak.

36. I am very weak both in the morning and afternoon.

37. I feel best after a good meal.

38. I feel very stuffy or sleepy after eating sweets and other starchy foods.

39. I am very sleepy during daytime.

40. I cannot sleep well during the night.

41. I wake up and cannot go back to sleep.

42. My sleep is deep but not refreshing.

43. I have cold sweats during the night.

44. I have no muscular strength upon awakening.

45. I need the stimulation of alcohol, coffee, cigarettes, or drugs.

46. I feel well after eating candy, cakes, or drinking soft drinks.

47. Alcohol, sweets and coffee make me feel very bad.

48. I have constipation.

49. I have alternating constipation and diarrhea.

50. I have abdominal distress.

51. I suffer from motion sickness.

52. I lost my appetite entirely.

53. Occasionally I am ravenously hungry.

54. I suffer from continuous indigestion.

55. I have frequent bloating.

56. A little alcohol makes me drunk.

57. I crave salt.

58. I have terrible headaches.

59. Occasionally I feel a pain across my left shoulder in the direction of my collar bone, or in the back of my neck.

60. I suffer from heat exhaustion.

61. I have swelling in my hands and feet.

62. My mouth is dry.

63. I have skin disease.

64. My hands perspire when I am excited.

65. My hands and legs feel cold.

66. I sweat exceedingly.

67. My skin is dry and scaly.

68. I perspire very little, except underarms, and the palms during stress.

69. My limbs feel numb.

70. I have a tingling feeling in my lips or fingers.

71. Sometimes I wake up in a sweat at night.

72. I have allergies, asthma.

73. My heart occasionally beats very fast.

74. Sometimes I tremble inside.

75. I catch a cold easily.

76. I am very susceptible to infectious diseases.

77. I have aching joints.

78. My muscles twitch occasionally.

79. Sometimes I have cramps.

80. I crave sweets and cakes, or pastry.

81. I do not drink much water.

82. I drink much coffee or tea every day.

83. I drink cola and other soft drinks daily.

84. I drink alcoholic beverages every day.

85. I am a chain-smoker.

Scoring: 25-30 or more indicates hypoglycemia

FEELINGS ASSESSMENT

Neurotransmitters enable communication to take place in the brain. While they all work, to an extent, in concert and not as individual chemical occurrences, it seems logical to think of "net" effects relating to overall results. In this way we can attribute certain thoughts, feelings and behaviors to "net" effects in neurotransmitter availability and performance.

Every thought, feeling and behavior is the result of, and results in, neurochemical equivalents in the brain.

We are attempting to group various thoughts, feelings and behaviors prevalent in hyperactive children or chemically depressed clients under the prominent neurotransmitter involved. An understanding of brain processes allows us to recommend actions to improve neurotransmitter availability enhancing the potential for positive thoughts, feelings and actions recovery.

Please check any and all feelings that are common to you:

Incomplete	O1	Difficult to have fun	D6
Shy	O2	Diminished spiritual concerns	D7
Needing Perfection - self/others	O3		
Unequal to others	O4	Lack of energy	N1
Not deserving	O5	Difficult to "get going"	N2
Something missing	O6	Decreased drive	N3
Low self worth or esteem	O7	Start projects and don't finish	N4
Inadequate	O8	Desires to sleep/hide	N5
Fearful	O9	Depressed	N6
		Paranoid	N7
Anxious for no reason	G1	Survival seems threatened	N8
"Free floating anxiety"	G2	Bored a great deal of the time	N9
Edgy, difficult to sit still	G3	Craving excitement	N10
"Knot" in stomach	G4	Seeking stimulation	N11
Difficulty falling asleep	G5		
Difficult to "turn off" my mind	G6	Sleep disturbance	S1
Panic—things closing in	G7	Irritable	S2
Thinks of alcohol/drug	G8	Lack of rational emotion	S3
to calm down		Sudden unexplained tears	S4
		Noise bothers you more than it	
Lack of pleasure in life	D1	used to. It seems louder.	S5
No real rewards in life	D2	"Flare up" at others	S6
Unexplained lack of concern		Unprovoked anger	S7
for others	D3	Depressed	S8
Decreased maternal/paternal		Unusually susceptible to pain	S9
feelings	D4	Want to be left alone	S10
Lack of "color" or "flavor" in		Problems focusing/concentrating	S11
your world	D5		

An Analysis of the Feelings Assessment

If you either have three answers checked in any one group or you have a total of ten checked overall, you have a possible deficiency of neurochemicals. The "raw materials", from which these chemicals are manufactured by the brain, are given as follows:

{ The D and N group can be increased through L-Phenylalanine supplementation.

{ The G group is increased with L-Glutamine supplementation.

{ The S group can be increased by taking 50 mg. of 5-HTP between meals.

{ The O group can be elevated with 500 mg. of D-Phenylalanine between meals.

D = Dopamine

N = Norepinephrine

G = GABA

S = Serotonin

O = Opiates

*** Used with permission of Dr. Terry Neher.

YEAST QUESTIONNAIRE

SECTION A: HISTORY   POINT SCORES

Circle your point scores.

1	Have you taken tetracycline's (Sumycin™, Panmycin™, Vibramycin™, Minocin™, etc.) or other antibiotics for acne for 1 month or longer?	35
2	Have you at any time in your life taken other broad-spectrum antibiotics (Keflex™, ampicillin, amoxicillin, Ceclor™, Bactrim™, Septra™) for respiratory, urinary or other infections (for two months or longer) or in shorter courses four or more times in a one year period?	35
3	Have you taken a broad-spectrum drug…even a single course?	6
4	Have you, at any time in your life, been bothered by persistent prostatitis, vaginitis or other problems affecting your reproductive organs?	25
5	Have you been pregnant.	
	2 or more times?	5
	1 time?	3
6	Have you taken birth control pills…	
	For more than 2 years?	15
	From 6 months to 2 years?	8
7	Have you taken prednisone, Decadron or other cortisone type drugs…	
	For more than 2 weeks?	15
	For 2 weeks or less?	8
8	Does exposure to perfumes, insecticides, fabric shop odors and other chemicals provoke…	
	Moderate to severe symptoms?	20
	Mild symptoms?	5
9	Are your symptoms worse on damp, muggy days or in moldy places?	20
10	Have you had athlete's foot, ringworm, "jock itch" or other chronic fungus infections of the skin or nails? Have such infections been…	
	Severe or persistent?	20
	Mild to moderate?	10
11	Do you crave sugar?	10
12	Do you crave bread?	10
13	Do you crave alcoholic beverages?	10
14	Does tobacco smoke really bother you?	10

TOTAL SCORE, SECTION A: _____

SECTION B: MAJOR SYMPTOMS:

For each of your symptoms, enter the appropriate figure in the Point Score column:

IF A SYMPTOM IS OCCASIONAL OR MILD	3 POINTS
IF A SYMPTOM IS FREQUENT AND/OR MODERATELY SEVERE	6 POINTS
IF A SYMPTOM IS SEVERE AND/OR DISABLING	9 POINTS

ADD THE TOTAL SCORE AND RECORD AT THE END OF THIS SECTION

SYMPTOM   POINT SCORE

1.   Fatigue or lethargy   _____
2.   Feeling of being drained   _____
3.   Poor memory   _____
4.   Feeling spacey or unreal   _____
5.   Inability to make decisions   _____
6.   Numbness, burning or tingling   _____
7.   Insomnia   _____
8.   Muscle aches   _____
9.   Muscle weakness or paralysis   _____
10. Pain and/or swelling in joints   _____
11. Abdominal pain   _____
12. Constipation   _____
13. Diarrhea   _____
14. Bloating, belching or intestinal gas   _____
15. Troublesome vaginal burning, itching or discharge   _____
16. Prostatitis   _____
17. Impotence   _____
18. Loss of sexual desire or feeling   _____
19. Endometriosis or infertility   _____
20. Cramps and/or other menstrual irregularities   _____
21. Premenstrual tension   _____
22. Attacks of anxiety or crying   _____
23. Cold hands or feet and/or chilliness   _____
24. Shaking or irritable when hungry   _____

TOTAL SCORE, SECTION B   _____

SECTION C: OTHER SYMPTOMS:

1.   Drowsiness _____
2.   Irritability or jitteriness _____
3.   Incoordination _____
4.   Inability to concentrate _____
5.   Frequent mood swings _____
6.   Headache _____
7.   Dizziness/loss of balance _____
8.   Pressure above ears...feeling of head swelling _____
9.   Tendency to bruise easily _____
10. Chronic rashes or itching _____
11. Numbness, tingling _____
12. Indigestion or heartburn _____
13. Food sensitivity or intolerance _____
14. Mucus in stools _____
15. Rectal itching _____
16. Dry mouth or throat _____
17. Rash or blisters in mouth _____
18. Bad breath _____
19. Foot, hair or body odor not relieved by washing _____
20. Nasal congestion or postnasal drip _____
21. Nasal itching _____
22. Sore throat _____
23. Laryngitis, loss of voice _____
24. Cough or recurrent bronchitis _____
25. Pain or tightness in chest _____
26. Wheezing or shortness of breath _____
27. Urinary urgency or frequency _____
28. Burning on urination _____
29. Spots in front of eyes or erratic vision _____
30. Burning or tearing of eyes _____
31. Recurrent infections or fluid in ears _____
32. Ear pain or deafness _____

TOTAL SCORE, SECTION C _____
TOTAL SCORE, SECTION A _____
TOTAL SCORE, SECTION B _____

GRAND TOTAL SCORE _____

Crook, William, The Yeast Connection Handbook, Professional Books, P. O. Box 3246, Jackson Tennessee, 38302, 1996, 1997.

YEAST QUESTIONNAIRE FOR CHILDREN

Circle the appropriate point score for questions you answer "yes." Total your score and record it at the end of the questionnaire.

Point Score

1. During the two years before your child was born, were you bothered by recurrent vaginitis, menstrual irregularities premenstrual tension, fatigue, headache, depression, digestive disorders or "feeling bad all over?"			30
2. Was your child bothered by thrush? (Score 10 if mild, score 20 if severe.)	10	20	
3. Was your child bothered by frequent diaper rashes in infancy? (Score 10 if mild, 20 if severe or persistent.)	10	20	
4. During infancy, was your child bothered by colic and irritability lasting over 30 months? (Score 10 if mild, 20 if moderate to severe.)			
5. Are his symptoms worse on damp days or in damp or moldy placed?		20	
6. Has your child been bothered by recurrent or persistent "athlete's foot" or chronic fungous infections of his skin or nails?			30
7. Has your child been bothered by recurrent hives, eczema or other skin problems?	10		
8. Has your child received:			60
a. 4 or more courses of antibiotic drugs during the past year? Or has he received continuous "prophylactic" courses of antibiotic drugs?			
b. 8 or more courses of "broad-spectrum" antibiotics (such as Keflex, amoxicillin, Septra, Bactrim or Ceclor) during the past three years?			40
9. Has your child experienced recurrent ear problems?		20	
10. Has your child had tubes inserted in his ears?	10		
11. Has your child been labeled "hyperactive"? (Score 10 if mild, 20 if moderate to severe.)	10	20	
12. Is your child bothered by learning problems (even though his early development history was normal)?	10		
13. Does your child have a short attention span?	10		
14. Is your child persistently irritable, unhappy and hard to please?	10		
15. Has your child been bothered by persistent or recurrent digestive problems, including constipation, diarrhea, bloating or excessive gas? (Score 10 if mild; 20 if moderate; 30 if severe)	10	20	30
16. Has he been bothered by persistent nasal congestion, cough and/or wheezing?	10		
17. Is your child unusually tired or unhappy or depressed? (Score 10 if mild, 20 if severe.)	10	20	

18. Has he been bothered by recurrent headaches, abdominal pain, or muscle aches? (Score 10 if mild, 20 if severe)	10	20	
19. Does your child crave sweets?	10		
20. Does exposure to perfume, insecticides, gas or other chemicals provoke moderate to severe symptoms?			30
21. Does tobacco smoke really bother him?		20	
22. Do you feel that your child isn't well, yet diagnostic tests and studies haven't revealed the cause?	10		
TOTAL SCORE			

Yeasts possibly play a role in causing health problems in children with scores of 60 or more.

Yeasts probably play a role in causing health problems in children with scores of 100 or more.

Yeasts almost certainly play a role in causing health problems in children with scores of 140 or more.

Crook, William, The Yeast Connection Handbook, Professional Books, P. O. Box 3246, Jackson Tennessee, 38302, 1996, 1997.

<u>THE LCP SOLUTION</u> JACQUELINE STORDY, Ph.D., and Malcolm Nicholl, Ballantine Books, New York, 2000. Amazon.com

SYMPTOMS OF OMEGA-3 FATTY ACID DEFICIENCY ARE:

TEMPER OUTBURSTS

VIOLENT BEHAVIOR

DOES NOT FINISH TASKS

IMPAIRED SHORT TERM MEMORY

POOR HANDWRITING, READING, SPEECH

SLEEP DISTURBANCE

FEAR OF THE DARK

POOR GROSS MOTOR COORDINATION

EXCESSIVE THIRST AND URINATION

ATTENTION DEFICIT DISORDER

LACK OF ENERGY

OBSESSIVE COMPULSIVE

HYPERACTIVE

DRY SKIN / ECZEMA

DEPRESSED

FEARFUL

FEW FRIENDS

ALLERGIES   (NOT BREAST FED AS AN INFANT)

CHAPTER 11

SUMMING UP

Hyperactive children are born with low serotonin, which may cause sleep disturbance, inattention, depression, unusual hunger, temper outbursts as well as sugar and alcohol cravings. They generally eat large amounts of sweets which can result in depression, fatigue, and depression of the immune system. Eating sweets may also impair the absorption of zinc, which is needed to activate many enzymes. Zinc is needed for growth, intellectual performance, the making of insulin, and sexual maturation. Hyperactive children may also begin life with fewer dopamine receptors and, hence, less dopamine, according to Kenneth Blum, Ph.D., a biochemist. This may very well increase the desire of the hyperactive youngster to drink alcohol.

Children who are hyperactive or have ADD generally have abnormal blood sugar, low levels of Omega-3 fatty acids and food allergies. Hair tissue analysis generally shows low levels of minerals, especially zinc, magnesium and chromium, and high levels of lead and cadmium. These children sometimes have low growth hormone.

Since the hyperactive child often suffers from exhaustion, low levels of blood sugar, inadequate supply of glucose in the brain, giving stimulants such as Ritalin would compound the problem.

What has been helpful to many hyperactive children is: taking specially formulated amino acid supplements, hypoallergenic vitamins, minerals, Omega-3 fatty acids, drinking filtered water and eating foods such as those suggested in Mastering the Zone or Zone Perfect Meals by Dr. Barry Sears. Children feel better when they get at least 30 minutes of sunlight (without glasses) each day, and take part in physical exercise and sports.

One of the children in my study suffered from visual disturbance, weakness and blackouts. Her first glucose tolerance test is found in Chapter 3 on page 37, example #25. Her test was stopped when her blood sugar went down to 55 mg %. She felt sick and could not continue the test.

For the next year, this girl omitted sugar, caffeine, and fruit juice from her diet. She ate fruits and vegetables, grains, lean meats, and took nutritional supplements. At the end of the year she repeated the glucose tolerance test. This time she completed the test. Her blood sugar had improved greatly, and she had no symptoms during the test. Her scores on the test were: F=85, 1/2=132, 1=132, 2=97, 3=85, 4=75, 5=74.

From the time she changed her diet and took the nutritional supplements, this thirteen year old girl did not have visual disturbance, weakness or blackouts again. This certainly demonstrates what Barry Sears says in <u>Mastering the Zone</u>: and <u>Omega Rx Zone</u>, that food selection can be a powerful tool to create health and well-being.

CHAPTER 12

WHAT TO DO... STEP BY STEP

a) Make extra copies of the Questionnaires in Chapter 10.

b) Answer the questions on each of the Questionnaires. Choose the appropriate Yeast Questionnaire.

c) Add the scores, placing the total in the top right-hand corner along with the date.

d) Answer the questions on the questionnaires again at the end of 6 weeks and again after 12 weeks.

e) Compare the scores on the Questionnaires.

As the scores go down, you should be seeing improvement in behavior, ability to concentrate, health and feeling states. You should see a happier person. Answer the Questionnaires at the end of each year. (You will not see improvement unless you make changes).

2. If your child is on Ritalin or another drug, take this book to your doctor and tell him that you would like to try another treatment. Ask his help by gradually withdrawing the Ritalin or other drug within one week's time. Ritalin keeps a child from eating and growing normally. It does not treat the underlying nutritional deficiencies. At the same time you withdraw the drug, follow Step 3 below.

3. Take 250-1,000 mg. Vitamin C and 1-2 beCalm'd three times a day between meals, depending on the age (see pages 67-74). The vitamin C should be buffered with alkaline minerals such as calcium, magnesium and potassium. You can order these from Bronson (800) 610-4848. #44 Chewable Vitamin C 250 mg. non-acidic; #83 Vitamin C 500 mg. (calcium ascorbate); #108 Vitamin C 1,000 mg. (calcium, ascorbate) or you can use another brand.

4. Take sugar and sugared foods such as sugared cereals, ice cream, cake, pies, candy bars, etc. out of your home. Replace these sweets with fresh fruits (except for bananas), dried fruits (except raisins) and canned fruits (canned in their own juice, not in heavy syrup).

5. Take sugared drinks such as: Kool Aid, soda pop, fruit juice out of your home. Replace with filtered water, herb tea sweetened with a small amount of Stevia Plus or Xylitol, club soda and fresh lemon, Perrier and lime, sparkling water, V-8 (in glass bottle), Clamato, Beefamato and fresh vegetable juice (if you have a juicer). Drink 6-10 8 ounce glasses of filtered water each 24 hours.

6. Eat breakfast, lunch and dinner with snacks in between meals. Eat protein and carbohydrate together at each meal. Examples of protein are: meat, cheese, whey protein and eggs. Examples of carbohydrates are: salads, vegetables, and fruits.

7. Take the vitamins, minerals, and essential fatty acids that are listed in Chapter 8, pages 68-76. Remember to take vitamins, minerals, fatty acids with food and beCalm'd between meals.

8. Get 30 minutes to 1 hour of sunlight each day without glasses. Do not look at the sun.

9. Do some exercise each day.

ADULTS	CHILDREN
30 minute fast walk	30 minute fast walk
Walk up and down stairs	Play soccer, baseball, basketball, football,
Play tennis or golf	Tennis
Swimming or aerobics	Swimming or aerobics
Lift weights	Participate in Boy/Girl Scouts, Campfire
Health Rider or other exercise machine	Girls
Dancing	Choir
	Activities sponsored by church, YMCA/YWCA

10. Stock up on foods containing unsaturated fats. These are: olives, olive oil, avocado, guacamole, almonds, slivered almonds, roasted peanuts, sugar free peanut butter, and Macadamia nuts. Eat small amounts of one of these with each meal.

11. Do not use sugar, fruit juice, cow's milk, dairy products, food coloring, and corn.

12. Stay away from pasta, bagels, rice and potatoes. See if you feel better and more energetic.

13. If you cannot sleep well, add 1-500 mg. tablet of GABA with the nutrients taken between 9:00 and 10:00 P.M. For people with depression, follow suggestions in Chapter 9 to raise serotonin.

14. When a child scores more than 100 on the Yeast Questionnaire for Children or an adult scores more than 100 on the Yeast Questionnaire, read The Yeast Connection Handbook and The Yeast Syndrome.

15. When you prepare vegetables, try buying them fresh, cutting them up, topping them with salt, pepper and oregano, then steaming them. Try broiling meats or cooking them in a little olive oil. Eat cold water fish 2-3 times a week (salmon, tuna, cod).

16. If you need professional help:

    - Ask your child's teacher to supervise his food choices.

    - Ask the school counselor to provide support.

    - Take this book to a nutritionally oriented physician or a Certified Clinical Nutritionist.

Warning: If you have the following symptoms: depression, thoughts of suicide, intense interest in sex, over-alert, lots of saliva, few caveties, obsessions, allergic reactions, use alcohol, drugs, sugar, or coffee to relieve symptoms, low pain threshold, or headaches, you may have high blood histamine (above 90 ng/ml, called histadelia). If so, you should not eat a high protein diet, take a multi vitamin, folic acid or B-12. Treatment should include:

1. Diet high in complex carbohydrates, moderate in fat, moderate in protein
2. 500 mg. L-Methionine 4 times a day
3. 25 mg. Zinc per day
4. 25 mg. Manganese per day
5. ½ tsp. Buffered powdered vitamin C or 2 1,000 mg. Capsules buffered C 3 times a day between meals
6. 120-240 mg. GLA 2 times a day

Reference: Jaffe, Russell and Kruesi, Oscar Rogers, "The Biochemical-Immunology Window: A Molecular View of Psychiatric Case Management", Journal of Applied Nutrition, Volume 44, Number 2, 1992.

To obtain a Hair Tissue Mineral Analysis including interpretation have your health care professional call Trace Elements in Addison, Texas at (800) 824-2314.